❦ The ❧
GREAT
CHARLES
DICKENS
SCANDAL

✦ MICHAEL SLATER ✦

YALE UNIVERSITY PRESS
NEW HAVEN AND LONDON

For information about this and other Yale University Press publications please contact:
U.S. Office: sales.press@yale.edu   www.yalebooks.com
Europe Office: sales@yaleup.co.uk   www.yalebooks.co.uk

Set in Adobe Caslon by IDSUK (DataConnection) Ltd
Printed in Great Britain by Hobbs The Printers, Totton, Hampshire

Library of Congress Cataloging-in-Publication Data

Slater, Michael.
    The great Charles Dickens scandal / Michael Slater.
        p. cm.
    Includes bibliographical references.
    ISBN 978–0–300–11219–1 (cl : alk. paper)
    1.   Dickens, Charles, 1812–1870—Relations with women.
    2.   Novelists, English—19th century—Biography.   I. Title.
    PR4582.S45 2012
    823'.8—dc23
    [B]

                                                            2012023963

A catalogue record for this book is available from the British Library.

ISBN 978-0-300-20528-2 (pbk)

10 9 8 7 6 5 4 3 2 1

For John Grigg

MICHAEL SLATER is Emeritus Professor of Victorian Literature at Birkbeck, University of London. He is a Past President of the International Dickens Fellowship and of the Dickens Society of America, Academic Adviser to the Board of Directors of the Charles Dickens Museum, London, and a former Editor of *The Dickensian*. His publications include *Dickens and Women* (1983), *An Intelligent Person's Guide to Dickens* (1999; reissued as *The Genius of Dickens*, 2012), *Douglas Jerrold 1803–1857* (2002), and *Charles Dickens* (2009). During 1994–2000 he edited *The Dent Uniform Edition of Dickens's Journalism* (4 vols; vol. 4 co-edited with John Drew). He has lectured on Dickens and other Victorian authors to a wide variety of audiences in North America, Europe, and in Japan where he was Visiting Professor at the University of Kyoto in 2005. He lives in London.

Contents

List of Illustrations

Acknowledgements

I would like to record here my grateful thanks to the following friends who kindly read all or part of this book in manuscript and from whose helpful and constructive comments I have greatly benefited: Dr Michael Baron and Robina Barson, Edward Costigan, Dr Jean Elliott, John Grigg, and Professor Toru Sasaki. I am grateful also to certain other friends – Professor John Drew, Q Love, Professor Jan Lokin and Pia Lokin, Chris Lungley and Dr Paul Schlicke – for their continued interest in this work and helpful talks about it, and to Professor Robert Bledsoe and Dr Elizabeth James for help with my research.

To Dr Patrick Leary I owe a special debt of gratitude for his very great generosity in sharing freely with me all the rich material he has assembled in the course of his extensive researches into nineteenth-century British and American newspaper coverage of the Dickens Scandal, and for allowing me to draw freely on it in this book. Dr Leary's essay on this subject will appear in *Charles Dickens and the Mid-Victorian Press 1850–1870*, ed. Hazel Mackenzie and Ben Winyard, University of Buckingham Press (forthcoming).

Once more I am indebted to Mark Dickens for his kindness in allowing me to quote from unpublished writings by members of the Dickens family. Every effort has been made to trace the current holders of other such material in the book as may still be in copyright.

I am grateful also to Professor Joel J. Brattin and to Michael Rogers for their excellent proof-reading.

Finally, it is a pleasure to record here, once again, my appreciation of all the help I have received during the writing of this book from the excellent staff of the wonderful Senate House Library of the University of London.

Introduction

... Charles Dickens, the man who committed what was in his lifetime considered incest with his wife's young sister. Poor Mrs Dickens was banished to a separate bedroom while her husband conducted many affairs, until he finally abandoned her and took their children with him. Nice guy.

Victoria Coren, *Observer Review*, 19 June 2002

Here is a sampling of Dickens-related headlines from the British press during the last ten years or so: 'THE DARK SIDE OF DICKENS AND THE LOVE THAT DESTROYED HIS MARRIAGE' (*Daily Mail*, 11 September 1999); 'DICKENS KEPT A KEEN EYE ON FALLEN WOMEN' (*Sunday Times*, 1 July 2001); 'DICKENS'S LOVER WAS HIDDEN IN A HOUSE BOUGHT BY THE AUTHOR' (*The Times*, 2 March 2005); 'NEW PLAY REVEALS A SCANDALOUS TWIST – HOW CHARLES DICKENS HAD A SECRET TEENAGE MISTRESS' (*Daily Mail*, 12 July 2007); 'THE SECRET AFFAIR THAT ALMOST RUINED DICKENS' (*Daily Telegraph*, 16 June 2008); 'DIAMOND RING COULD PROVE DICKENS HAD SECRET LOVE-CHILD' (*Daily Telegraph*, 5 February 2010); 'REVEALED: THE TEENAGE MISTRESS WHO MESMERISED

CHARLES DICKENS . . . AND BROKE HIS WIFE'S HEART' (*Daily Mail*, 21 May 2010); 'CALAIS LAYS CLAIM TO DICKENS VIA HIS SECRET SPICY CHAPTER' (*The Times*, 31 May 2011). Most eye-catching of all, as might be expected, was the *Sunday Sport*'s 'DICKENS'S ROMPS WITH NAUGHTY NELLY', the headline with which it greeted the publication of Claire Tomalin's *The Invisible Woman: The Story of Nelly Ternan and Charles Dickens* in the autumn of 1990.

The rest of these attention-grabbing headlines (several of which appeared under the convenient all-purpose banner-headline 'WHAT THE DICKENS!') also need some explanation. In 1999 *The Daily Mail* was wanting to spice up its report of the sale at auction by the Dickens family of Dickens's business archive of contracts with his publishers. In 2001 *The Sunday Times* was reporting the discovery of some new letters relating to Dickens's involvement with a 'Home For Homeless Women' – nearly always more thrillingly referred to nowadays, even by scholars, as a 'Home For Fallen Women' – set up by millionaire philanthropist Angela Burdett Coutts. In 2005 *The Times* was commenting on the newly-published 1861 census returns. In 2007 *The Daily Mail* was previewing Simon Gray's play *Little Nell*. In 2008 *The Daily Telegraph* was reviewing a TV 'docudrama' about Dickens and Ellen Ternan. In 2010 the same paper was reporting on a provincial auction which featured an engraved diamond ring that, so it was claimed, had once belonged to a love-child born to Dickens and his young sister-in-law Georgina Hogarth. The *Daily Mail* headline of the same year captioned a piece by A. N. Wilson commenting on the news that a film was to be made about Dickens and Ellen Ternan 'which will bring their extraordinary story to wider attention'. *The Times* was writing about a Dickens exhibition in the Pas de Calais region of France, not far from a 'love nest' the writer had supposedly had in the village of Condette.

We noted the *Sunday Sport*'s headline was inspired by the publication of Claire Tomalin's *The Invisible Woman*. This book's great success owed much, of course, to its author's established reputation as an accomplished and highly readable biographer. It also undoubtedly owed something to the public's apparently endless fascination with Dickens's love life, more especially with his sex life. This leads journalists and scholars, as well as some creative writers, to revisit again and again the subject of the departure from the marital home of his wife of twenty years and Dickens's subsequent twelve-year secret relationship with a young woman from the world of the professional theatre who was born in the same year as his second daughter.

What is the reason for this fascination? Surely it is rooted in the fact that Dickens is, like Shakespeare, Jane Austen and Thomas Hardy, one of our great 'National Treasure' authors, giants of the so-called 'heritage industry'. His work, and the dramatic story of his life, still attracts large audiences across different media because, as John Sutherland expressed it in *The Financial Times* in March 2009, he is a figure 'deeply embedded in our national psyche'. This has much to do, of course, with the fact that he is our great national celebrant of hearth, home and family love. Of all the scenes and episodes in English literature, the Cratchit family's humble Christmas dinner in *A Christmas Carol* is undoubtedly one of the most familiar and best-loved. Radiant domesticity is also the dominant mood at the end of most of his great novels, notably the strongly autobiographical *David Copperfield*. More generally, Dickens can be said to represent for us today the benign face of those 'Victorian values' once so memorably invoked by Margaret Thatcher. Any association of him and his work with the even remotely salacious is therefore bound to have for us an interest that seems destined never to lose its piquant savour.

Charles Dickens became a major celebrity in his early twenties, first on the national stage and very quickly afterwards on the international one, and he remained so until his untimely death at the age of fifty-eight. As a result, an almost overwhelming amount of documentary evidence is available to us today, about both his private and his public life. The definitive edition of his surviving letters runs to twelve stout volumes, and there are innumerable reminiscences of him which were published by his family, friends, colleagues and acquaintances. There are dozens of biographies. He and his works were, moreover, the subject of endless column-inches in the newspapers and journals that proliferated in the 'age of periodicals', as Wilkie Collins once called the Victorian era. Despite all this, however, there still remain tantalising gaps in our knowledge of many aspects of his life, most particularly as regards his relations with women. We know many *facts* about these relationships but the interpretation of those facts has, from his own day onwards, been a lively subject for gossip, conjecture and debate, and in more recent times, for detailed scholarly research. To none of such relationships does this apply more fully than to his connection, for the last twelve years of his life, with the young actress Ellen Ternan, always known as Nelly.

In 1858 the gossip, fuelled by Dickens's own wild indiscretion, quickly spread across the Atlantic, where, too, he was seen as the great champion of hearth and home (and where libel laws were a good deal less stringent than in Britain). Gradually, the gossip diminished, on both sides of the Atlantic, mainly for want of matter to feed upon. For over seventy years the vigilance of, first, Dickens himself, and then, after his death, of his immediate family, managed to keep scandalous rumour pretty much stifled, thereby maintaining his highly bankable image as not only a supremely great writer but also as a truly good and pure man. In 1928, however, a poor novel called *This Side Idolatry* painted a very different picture of him, thereby causing a great sensation in the literary world. Six years later the death of Dickens's last surviving child led directly to a blazing revival of the scandal – initially, bizarrely enough, as part of a fierce circulation battle then being fought between two of Britain's mass-circulation daily papers. Since that time it has periodically flared up again, in one form or another, as new information regarding their relationship has come to light. In the following pages I seek to trace the main outlines of this history.

Prologue

Dickens in 1857

When Dickens celebrated his forty-fifth birthday on 7 February 1857 he had been for twenty years the favourite story-teller of the English-speaking world. His novels, from *Pickwick Papers* onwards, and his series of Christmas Books, beginning with the immortal *A Christmas Carol* in 1843, had sold and continued to sell in such vast quantities that Anthony Trollope once jokingly wrote that he thought they must be consumed in families like loaves of bread or joints of beef. Since 1850 he had 'conducted' a weekly journal, *Household Words*, which sold for two pence, thus making it affordable by a wide range of lower middle- and working-class readers. It further strengthened the ties between him and his public, especially as he himself was a regular contributor, with articles ranging from entertaining sketches and familiar essays to fiercely satirical ones that focused on various contentious social issues.

In private life he had for just over twenty years been, to all outward appearances, happily married to Catherine, née Hogarth, a kindly, gentle woman who seems to have been greatly liked by everyone who met her, and who had borne him ten children, seven boys and three girls. The youngest girl, Dora, had died in infancy in 1851. The eldest child, Charles, was twenty years old in 1857 and Dickens was trying to get him settled in a career. The youngest boy, Edward, always known as Plorn, was just five. Throughout all the years of his marriage Dickens's imagination seems to have been haunted by memories of two women other than Catherine. The first was the pretty, petite and apparently somewhat coquettish banker's daughter, Maria Beadnell, whom he had passionately but vainly wooed when he was between the ages of eighteen and twenty-one and who had come near to breaking his heart. He had painted an idealised picture of her as Dora in his semi-autobiographical novel *David Copperfield*, written in 1849–50. The second was Mary Hogarth, Catherine's younger sister, who appears to have been a notably charming, sympathetic and sweet-natured girl. She stayed with Dickens and Catherine in the very earliest days of their marriage and her sudden death in 1837, aged seventeen, had been a devastating shock to them both. Catherine's next youngest sister, Georgina, had joined the Dickens household in 1842 when she was fifteen in order to help Catherine look after the growing band of children. Dickens appreciated Georgina's domestic competence and enjoyed her company, and together with Catherine and Georgina – his 'pair of petticoats' as he liked to call them – he formed a very successful domestic and social unit. Friends and acquaintances got used to meeting Georgina as a maiden-aunt fixture in the Dickens household. Thackeray, for example, wrote to his mother about meeting Dickens on the pier at Ryde with his wife, his children and 'his Miss Hogarth' (they all, he wrote, looked 'abominably coarse, vulgar and happy').

John Forster, Dickens's most intimate friend from early manhood onwards and his first biographer, tells us that it was in 1854 that Dickens first began confiding in him about 'home dissatisfactions and misgivings'. Comparing himself to his own

David Copperfield, he asked, 'Why is it that, as with poor David, a sense comes always crushing on me now, when I fall into low spirits, as of one happiness I have missed in life, and one friend and companion I have never made?' This state of mind helps to explain the extraordinary intensity of Dickens's response in February 1855 when Maria Beadnell, now Mrs Henry Winter and not seen by him for many years, suddenly wrote to him out of the blue. Unable to see her immediately, he plunged into a fervent secret correspondence with her, arranging to meet her again when nobody else was by, and recalling in astonishing detail, and with much serio-comic pity for his younger self, all his former devotion to her. The instant disillusionment that resulted when he actually beheld the hapless object of his former passion, now florid, fat and forty-four, no doubt contributed greatly to that growing sense of restlessness and private unhappiness about which he wrote to Forster – also, no doubt, to that undertone of sadness that the reader feels in the great novel on which he was then working, *Little Dorrit*, which was in many respects a good deal more ruthlessly autobiographical than *David Copperfield*.

During the latter part of 1856 while he continued with the writing of *Little Dorrit*, Dickens was also collaborating with his younger friend and fellow-writer Wilkie Collins on a melo-drama entitled *The Frozen Deep*. A full-scale production of this play, with a cast made up of Collins and other friends, plus Georgina Hogarth and Dickens's daughters, Mary and Katey, was elaborately staged at Dickens's home Tavistock House in January. Dickens both directed the production and acted the leading role. He gave a truly sensational performance as Richard Wardour, a man of intense passions who, in the Arctic wastes where the main action of the drama is set, sacrifices his own life in order to save that of the younger man who, unwittingly, is his successful rival in love. Having achieved this sublime act, Wardour is given a tremendous death scene which has him expiring in the arms of the woman he has so greatly loved. When the performances were over, Dickens sorely missed the cathartic excitement of them, even though he had a few other things to distract him like finishing *Little Dorrit* and all the business involved in the purchase of his first freehold property, Gad's Hill Place in Kent. Then in June 1857 the sudden death of his much-loved old friend, the writer Douglas Jerrold, gave him the chance to revive *The Frozen Deep* as part of a series of fund-raising events he decided to organise for the benefit of Jerrold's widow and unmarried daughter. A Royal Command Performance was given before Queen Victoria and Prince Albert, followed by three public performances, all in a comparatively intimate venue called the Gallery of Illustration. Once again, audiences were completely overwhelmed by the power of Dickens's Wardour. It was decided to take the production to the great Free Trade Hall in Manchester and as a result it became necessary to recruit professional actresses capable of projecting their voices so as to be heard in such a vast auditorium. Determined to get 'the best who *have been* upon the stage', Dickens was delighted to be able to hire Frances Eleanor Ternan, a distinguished theatrical veteran who had acted with the great Macready himself, and her two younger daughters, Maria and Ellen. Maria, already an accomplished actress, played the heroine Clara while eighteen-year-old Ellen, who professionally was just beginning to take on adult roles, played a minor part. However, in the farce *Uncle John* that, following contemporary practice, was given as an after-piece she got to play opposite Dickens as the object of his amorous attentions.

Once the Manchester performances were over, *Little Dorrit* successfully concluded, and the activities on behalf of the Jerrold Fund (which had also included Dickens giving hugely successful public readings of *A Christmas Carol* to vast audiences both in London and Manchester) finished, Dickens found himself in a

9

desperate state, feeling 'as if the scaling of all the Mountains of Switzerland . . . would be but a slight relief'. He persuaded Collins to come with him on a jaunt to the North of England, ostensibly to collaborate in writing a series of travel pieces for *Household Words* called 'The Lazy Tour of Two Idle Apprentices'. The primary purpose, it would seem, was to provide a pretext for being in Doncaster during the September Races Week when, he knew, the Ternans had an engagement at the theatre there. Ellen is anonymously celebrated in a rhapsodic passage in 'The Lazy Tour' describing a beautiful golden-haired wearer of a 'winning little bonnet' seen at the races. In the previous instalment of this series Dickens had powerfully described a husband successfully *willing* his wife to death ('she had long been in the way, and he had long been weary'). He is spied on by a very young man who passionately loves her, 'a slender youth . . . with long light-brown hair', like the young Dickens. This youth is powerless to save her but at once confronts the murderer, who then kills him too, in a sort of trance. Unlike the golden-haired beauty at the races, the woman in this story does have a name. It is Ellen.

Meanwhile Dickens's letters home from the tour were all being written to Georgina, not to Catherine, while in the letters he wrote to Forster he reverted to his domestic woes:

> Poor Catherine and I are not made for each other. . . . Her temperament will not go with mine. . . . What is now befalling me I have seen steadily coming on, ever since the days you remember when Mary [his eldest daughter, born in 1838] was born; and I know too well that you cannot, and no one can help me.

Thus was Dickens writing about his emotional state in 1857, indirectly in 'The Lazy Tour' and directly to Forster. In this same year the writing was also, figuratively speaking, upon the wall.

CHAPTER ONE

1858
Enter rumour

As Thackeray was going into the Garrick Club one evening in late May 1858 he was greeted by some fellow-members eager to know if he had heard the sensational news that Dickens, after more than twenty years of marriage and the begetting of ten children, had separated himself from his wife Catherine. It was, they claimed, the result of an 'intrigue' between Dickens and his resident sister-in-law Georgina Hogarth, Catherine's junior by eleven years. This was a very grave charge indeed – a question not just of adultery, which would have been bad enough, but of what would then have been legally classified as incest. Describing the incident in a letter to his mother, Thackeray ruefully admitted that in seeking to defend Dickens from this hugely damaging accusation, he had let quite another cat out of the bag: 'No such matter', he told the gossips, 'It's with an actress'.

Well might his clubmen friends have been excited. The news of the breakdown of Dickens's marriage had come as a complete shock to the public. Many of his devoted readers, commented J. Hain Friswell in his *Charles Dickens: A Critical Biography* published this very year, 'seeing that "David Copperfield" was in form autobiographical, and was actually so in some parts, have amused themselves with speculations in the matter of Mr Dickens's married life'. Now, he continued, alluding to certain statements about the end of his marriage that, as we shall see, were imprudently issued by Dickens, 'a rough solution has been afforded by Mr Dickens himself, who tells us that his marriage to Miss Hogarth was not productive of happiness to either of them'. Inevitably, Georgina became the target of gossip when, following her sister's sad departure from the marital home accompanied only by Charley the eldest son, she stayed on to run Dickens's household for him and to take care of the younger children – in conjunction with his eldest daughter, twenty-year-old Mary, or 'Mamie' as she was always called. Catherine Dickens herself was, as it were, pensioned off ('dismissed with a good character', commented one of the wags on the staff of the comic weekly *Punch*) with £600 a year, a brougham, and a 'pretty little house' in Gloucester Crescent, not far from Regent's Park. Meanwhile Dickens was naturally anxious that this upheaval in his domestic life should not adversely affect the – potentially highly lucrative – new career on which he was just then embarking, giving public readings from his own works. He had been heartened by the tremendous warmth of his reception on the occasion of his first commercial reading – of, as it happens, his intensely domestic little Christmas Book *The Cricket on the Hearth* – at St Martin's Hall, Long Acre, on 29 April, but this had been before the news broke in early May of his separation from Catherine.

Now, on 25 May, while negotiations regarding Catherine's settlement were still pending, Dickens provided his readings manager Arthur Smith, a much-loved and trusted friend, with a statement about the separation, together with a covering note giving Smith full permission to show it to 'any one who wishes to do me right, or who may have been misled into doing me wrong'. This was what Dickens later came to refer to as 'the Violated Letter' (see Appendix 2). In producing it he had in mind, no doubt, those who might have fought shy of the readings having heard sensational gossip about his private life. In the statement he asserts that there had always been a basic incompatibility of character and temperament between Catherine and himself. With notable lack of compunction, he then goes on to describe her as a failed mother who threw all the care of her children on to Georgina (for whom, he says, they all have 'the tenderest affection') and even to assert that Catherine was sometimes mentally unbalanced. He refers darkly to 'two wicked persons' who have blamed the separation upon his involvement with 'a young lady' for whom he has 'a great attachment and regard'. He will not name her, he says, but roundly proclaims: 'Upon my soul and honour, there is not on this earth a more virtuous and spotless creature than this young lady. I know her to be innocent and pure, and as good as my own dear daughters.'

The result of this document as it got into circulation was, of course, merely to arouse curiosity and provoke questions. Just who, for example, were those 'two wicked persons' who should have spoken of Dickens very differently, 'in consideration of earned respect and gratitude'? This was soon answered when another document, signed by Catherine's mother, Mrs George Hogarth, and by her youngest daughter, Helen, was appended to this letter to Smith. In this addendum, which Dickens had absolutely demanded should be produced, Mrs Hogarth and Helen repudiated 'certain statements' indicating that the separation had resulted from 'circumstances deeply affecting the moral character of Mr Dickens', a reference, presumably, to the gossip about him and Georgina. But who was the radiantly pure young lady referred to in the penultimate paragraph of Dickens's statement? The chattering classes of the day did not have far to look for a likely candidate given the recent involvement of Frances Eleanor Ternan and her two younger daughters, Maria and Ellen, all three of them professional actresses, in Dickens's amateur company's production of Wilkie Collins's melodrama *The Frozen Deep*.

It hardly needed Thackeray's indiscretion, therefore, to set the scandalmongers on the Ternans' trail. In the letter to his mother already quoted Thackeray says that he first heard about Dickens's actress from 'a man at Epsom'. Could this perhaps have been some devotee of the turf who had noticed Dickens at Doncaster Races the previous September when Maria and Ellen, chaperoned by their mother, had been engaged at the theatre there and Dickens had been dancing attendance on the family? There certainly was, Thackeray continued, 'some row about an actress in the case' but Dickens was denying 'with the utmost infuriation' any charge against her or himself. He has not yet, Thackeray adds, seen Dickens's statement, meaning the letter Dickens gave to Arthur Smith, but he has evidently learned the details in it from someone who has. Smith, it seems, wasted no time in showing the document around. He was prompted, no doubt, by his zeal to counteract what Georgina called, in a letter of 31 May pretty clearly dictated by Dickens, to Dickens's old flame Maria Winter, 'the most wonderful and wicked rumours which have been flying about the town'. (Mrs Winter, as we have seen, had three years before had startling evidence of Dickens's capacity for sudden emotional turbulence and, aware of this, he would surely have been concerned to keep her as calm as possible in this crisis in his domestic life.)

One choice bit of gossip that was circulating in the metropolis was learned by Hans Christian Andersen away in Denmark, where he was still nursing fond memories of his five-week visit to the Dickens household the previous summer during which he had apparently been quite oblivious of any domestic tensions.

A friend of his, the painter Elisabeth Jerichau-Baumann, wrote to him from London about what she had heard concerning the cause of the break between Dickens and Catherine:

D. had sent a bracelet with a poem to an actress; it got lost, and D. advertised for it in the papers. It was sent, his wife received it, thinking it was a present for her; she put it on, the poem fell out – and she never forgave him that after having been married to her for 25 years [actually, 21] he could enter into an understanding with another.

Dickens himself was at this time in a highly combustible state, incensed by what he called in a letter written on 31 May to the novelist Catherine Gore 'such thronging multitudes of wonderful and inexplicable lies about myself'. They posed a distinct threat to the success of the readings and to that special relationship he had with his hundreds of thousands of devoted readers which he once described to Forster as 'personally affectionate and like no other man's'. To counteract this threat he decided to publish his side of the story in a far more effective way than just having Smith show the document he had given him to various individuals. He drew up a second statement headed 'Personal' which, overriding the strenuous objections of many friends including Forster, he caused to be published in *The Times* on 7 June and in his own weekly magazine *Household Words* a few days later (see Appendix 1). In it he spoke in general terms of 'some domestic trouble of mine, of long-standing . . . of a sacredly private nature' which had 'now been brought to an arrangement' and 'amicably composed' ('Alas', commented the Sunday journal *John Bull* on 12 June, 'for the trouble that can be brought to so easy an arrangement! Alas for the twenty years of wedded life that can be amicably composed, so that nothing is left but for their details to be forgotten!').

In his concern to protect both Georgina and Ellen, Dickens again referred to unnamed third parties who were being traduced ('innocent persons dear to my heart, and innocent persons of whom I have no knowledge'). He 'most solemnly' declared, both in his own name and in Catherine's, her consent having been obtained (not that she had much choice in the matter), that all such rumours were 'abominably false'. As with the earlier document he had given to Arthur Smith, this statement served only to stir up more gossip and wild rumours, blazoning the matter the length and breadth of the country. Some papers were simply bemused, or pretended to be. 'Now really', commented *The Critic* on 12 June, 'we should be very much obliged to anybody who will inform us – what this is all about? What are the "misrepresentations"? What are the "slanders" . . . ?' A few weeks later, on 3 July, the journal reverted to the matter, referring to 'the error into which Mr Dickens fell when he put forward that extraordinary document which, as we predicted . . . has set all the old women in the land inquiring into what dreadful things the amiable author of "Pickwick" has been doing'. *The Morning Post* was clear that the accusation brought against Dickens was one of 'gross profligacy' and this highly aristocratic newspaper, normally no friend to Dickens, now championed him on 7 June as the author of works 'utterly free from any taint or stain of vice'. The slanderous 'poison', said the *Post*, mixing its metaphors rather freely, had been spread abroad by 'the hundred tongues of Fame' and it rejoiced that Dickens 'has stepped forward like a man, at whatever cost to his feelings, to brush away the web of untruth, and to claim the belief due to candour and innocence'.

At the other end of the social spectrum of the English press from *The Morning Post* were papers like the cheekily-named *Court Circular*, which gleefully reported on 12 June the scabrous rumour that Dickens had preferred 'his wife's sister to herself, a preference which has assumed a very definite and tangible shape', and the widely-circulated *Reynolds's Weekly Newspaper*. The editor of the latter was G. W. M. Reynolds, an amazingly prolific writer of cheap sensational fiction. He had done well out of plagiarising Dickens at the outset of his writing career with publications like his *Pickwick in America*, but now owed him a grudge for having been denounced in the 'Preliminary Word' to *Household Words* (30 March 1850) as 'a Pander to the basest passions of the lowest natures'. He seized on the publication of Dickens's personal statement to attack him in the 13 June issue of his *Weekly Newspaper*:

> The names of a female relative, and of a professional young lady, have both been, of late, so freely and intimately associated with that of Mr Dickens as to excite suspicion and surprise in the minds of those who had hitherto looked upon the popular novelist as a very Joseph in all that regards morality, chastity and decorum.

And he returned to the charge a week later noting that 'the rumours that are now afloat about this unhappy affair are innumerable'. These rumours were denounced by the gossip columnist Edmund Yates in the 19 June issue of his magazine *Town Talk* as 'lies so preposterous in their malice, as almost to defeat the design of their concocters', yet Dickens, he claimed, had been obliged publicly to deny them as they involved the names of 'most innocent and worthy persons'.

A year later George Augustus Sala, who like Yates was one of 'Dickens's young men', as certain staffers on *Household Words* were called, was mischievously to remind his colleague of an epigram that was doing the rounds of literary London in this summer of 1858:

With tongue and pen few can like Dickens fudge
But now in vain for virtue's cause he pleads –
The world *his* virtues in the end will judge
Not by his Household Words, but Household Deeds.

Meanwhile the news had sped across the Atlantic. On 18 June *The New York Herald* published a long piece mailed to it by its London correspondent on 4 June asserting that it was 'all fudge' to say that Dickens and his wife were separating after twenty-two years of marriage on account of 'incompatibility of temper'. The real cause was the coming into Dickens's life, as a result of his fund-raising amateur dramatic activities in which it 'was necessary to get some histrionic talent beyond the benevolent projectors', of 'a Miss Ternan, well known in Manchester, and latterly on the London boards'. A 'very pure and very platonic affection' had sprung up between her and 'the author of Pickwick', but she was now 'charged with being the cause of the separation that has just taken place between the eminent author and his wife'. Three days later *The New York Times* published a report dated 8 June from its London correspondent: 'All London, you must know, had for some time been rife with legends concerning Dickens and an actress, with whom it was at last affirmed that the author of David Copperfield had eloped to Boulogne. . . . He has indeed separated from his wife, but only on account of an ancient and unconquerable incompatibility in their respective characters'.

The correspondents of the New York papers seem to have been unaware that there were no fewer than three Misses Ternan extant. In England only the eldest, Fanny (also an actress but, ironically, the one member of the family who had *not* acted with Dickens), could properly be referred to as 'Miss Ternan', so these newspaper references led, as will be seen below, to some confusion on the part of the Ternans' American relatives.

The *Herald*'s correspondent added: 'Dickens does not get much sympathy, the public generally deciding, as it does usually in such cases, in favour of the lady'. Another New York paper, the popular weekly *Frank Leslie's Illustrated Newspaper*, threw its net rather wider and did display some sympathy with Dickens, albeit of a somewhat coarse and distasteful kind. The first paragraph in its 'Gossip of the World' column on 3 July reads as follows:

Charles Dickens. – This great author, whose works have humanised the present age to so great an extent, has separated from his wife. The reasons are variously stated. Some of his enemies say it is an unfortunate *penchant* for actresses; others that Mrs Milner Gibson [wife of a prominent Liberal politician and a notable London hostess] led his fancy astray. As Dickens is forty-seven [*sic*], and Mrs Gibson forty-five, we think the similarity of years would neutralise the similarity of tastes. Miss Ternan has also been mentioned, and Miss Amy Sedgwick, both of them actresses. It is to be regretted that after having endured his wife for twenty-five years [actually twenty-two], he could not hold on a little longer. Twenty-five years ago Katharine [*sic*] Hogarth was as pretty a young woman as ever changed her name, and tolerably amiable. She was, however, constitutionally indolent and unintellectual. In addition to this, she had a tendency to corpulency, which is very disgusting to a man of elegant tastes, or who has much company at home, since it materialises the head of his table, and converts the high priestess of the repast into the fattest joint on the board.

The writer goes on to report gossip about the tangled marital affairs of two other literary figures, G. H. Lewes, George Eliot's consort since 1854, and Thornton Hunt. This report is attributed to Charles Mackay, editor of *The Illustrated London News*, 'during his recent visit to America'. It may be that Mackay was also the source for the gossip about Dickens, though this seems unlikely given that the *News*, in defending his publication of his 'Personal' statement on 12 June, had referred to Dickens's well-known 'noble nature' as sufficient grounds for accepting his account of the situation. Not everyone, however, agreed about the 'nobility' of Dickens's nature, as is shown by a spiteful letter in the archives of the Royal Literary Fund written by Newton Crosland, one of the leading opponents of Dickens's vigorous but unsuccessful campaign to reform the administration of the Fund. Dickens appealed in his 'Personal' statement to his own 'known character as some evidence in my favour'. Alluding to this, Crosland writes, 'I must confess I do not feel the weight and importance of your denial, as my general knowledge of your character induced me to believe that certain obnoxious rumours against you were true when I heard them about ten days ago, at the corner of every street and in every social circle'.

Meanwhile, more gossip and scandal was crossing the Atlantic. On 22 June *The Detroit Free Press* published a 'letter from London' containing a version of the misdirected jewels anecdote retailed to Andersen by Jerichau-Baumann:

I hear that Dickens has for some time been paying attention to an actress at the Haymarket (Amy Sedgwick, it is thought). So charmed was he that he went to Hunt & Roskell's and bought her a beautiful bracelet . . . and had the lady's name engraved upon it. The trinket was unfortunately lost one night when he was taking her to a place of amusement and was found by some honest person, who took it to Hunt & Roskell's, who at once sent it to Mr Dickens, and as Mr Dickens was out, Mrs Dickens received the naughty tell-tale. She presented it to her lord when he came home, and simply said, 'Charles I wish you would not be so open in these matters,' whereupon . . . the editor of Household Words went into a towering passion, and said he would not stay another minute in the same house with his wife. . . .

Very different was the reason for the rift between Dickens and Catherine given in *The Boston Atlas and Bee* and copied into *The New York Times* of 29 June. A correspondent of the paper reported that he had been talking to someone who knew the Dickens family well, and the disagreement between Dickens and his wife stemmed from the 'diverse views' they took 'in regard to the religious education of their daughters', Dickens being 'a decided latitudinarian' in religion while Catherine was a strict Presbyterian. Other American papers ascribed the cause of the marital breakdown variously to Catherine's not being 'intellectual' and so not appreciating her husband's work (*Charleston Courier*, 20 July) or to Dickens becoming tired of her and her lack of ambition as he basked in 'the dazzling enchantment of Lords and Ladies' (*Daily Cleveland Herald*, 20 July).

Britain's libel laws ensured that gossip appearing in the American press would not be reproduced on the British side of the Atlantic, but there was nothing to prevent British newspapers from reprinting Dickens's own words once his open letter to Arthur Smith had been published in America. The earliest printing of it seems to have been in *The New York Herald* on 15 August, from where it was copied into *The New York Tribune* for 16 August. In a magisterial editorial reproof of Dickens printed in the same issue, the *Tribune* points out the significance of the fact that Catherine Dickens had remained entirely silent about the separation and its causes:

There is no impeachment of Mr Dickens's conduct . . . resting upon any authority whatever. That lying rumour should be busy with the case . . . was inevitable. Every libertine in Anglo-Saxondom, male or female, is sure of course that there is another lady in the case, if not several ladies. Mr Dickens was stung by the circulation of anonymous scandals to publish, through 'Household Words', his solemn, emphatic denial that there was any shadow of foundation for such scandals. There he should have stopped. Nobody but his wife should have had power to call him out again. Yet he has been tempted to write again, ostensibly for private circulation only, but his letter has got into print, as such letters always will. We shall not criticise it; we only insist that he could say nothing that would be so advantageous to him as silence. In a case of matrimonial abrasion, the public sympathy instinctively takes the side of the weaker party – that is, the wife – unless she persists in proving herself a vulgar shrew and virago like Lady Bulwer [estranged wife of Edward Bulwer-Lytton, who plagued him by turning up and denouncing him on public occasions]; but where the wife maintains perfect silence and the husband issues bulletin after bulletin, he is sure to lose ground with each succeeding hour. One more uncalled-for letter from Mr. D. will finish him.

The first appearance in the English press of the 'Violated Letter', as Dickens always subsequently called this document (though he appears never to have blamed Smith for its entering the public domain), seems to have been in *The Morning Star* for 30 August. The *Star* in its editorial comment on the document noted that it

contains a very broad statement, to the effect that MRS DICKENS entirely neglected the care of her children, without, however, any further particulars on that point, except that her sister GEORGINA . . . has performed the duties to the children which MRS DICKENS neglected. The public will, of course, bear in mind that in this painful case MRS DICKENS has all along remained silent. Her husband's story only has been told. It is possible that she might, if disposed, put a different complexion upon it.

Other papers featured more severe critical editorial comment, as *The New York Tribune* had done. *The Liverpool Mercury*, for example, in a long piece entitled 'The Literary Man and the Public', cited Dickens's words about 'the manly consideration towards Mrs Dickens which I owe to my wife' and comments:

> This favourite of the public informs some hundreds of thousands of readers that the wife whom he has vowed to love and cherish has utterly failed to discharge the duties of a mother; and he further hints that her mind is disordered. If this is 'manly consideration' we should like to be favoured with a definition of unmanly selfishness and heartlessness.
>
> [9 September 1858]

More than a month before the 'Violated Letter' appeared in the British press, Dickens's inaugural series of professional readings at St Martin's Hall had ended (22 July). They had been a huge success and the public's adulation of the reader seems to have been entirely unaffected by the recent sensation concerning his domestic life. So it was also with his first readings tour, which between August and November took him all over England as well as to Scotland and Ireland. Writing to Georgina from Exeter on 5 August, and no doubt wanting to reassure her especially about the ineffectuality of the scandalmongers, he said he had never seen anything like 'the personal affection which they poured out upon me at the end' (*Chambers's Exeter Journal* had on 7 August reprobated the 'vile poisonous calumny' that continued to be whispered against him by 'reptiles who bite at his heel') and he made a similar report to her from Dublin on 29 August. Even after the 'Violated Letter' had appeared and he had, according to Forster, been the subject of unfavourable comment in a Manchester paper, he could still write to Forster (20/21 September) that the welcome his audience had given him there 'was astounding in its affectionate recognition of the late trouble', though it is not quite clear whether this was a matter of belief or of certain knowledge on his part.

Earlier (23 August) Dickens had been keen to let Angela Burdett Coutts know that large numbers of clergymen attended his readings. No doubt he hoped thereby to reassure this devoutly Anglican millionairess, for whom he acted as unofficial almoner and who was less than happy about his treatment of Catherine, that he was still very much countenanced by the Church. On 24 September *The Aberdeen Free Press* devoted two weighty columns to discussing the collapse of the Dickens marriage and the 'Violated Letter', expressing grave disquiet that Dickens should advance 'incompatibility' as a sufficient reason for separating himself from his wife:

> When we hear of separations taking place on the ground of 'incompatibility', it leads us to suspect there is something radically wrong in the training, the temper, or the conduct of one or other of the parties – probably enough of both. At the least, it is a proof of moral cowardice on the side – whichever – where the demand for separation comes.

Despite such adverse press comment, Dickens's audiences in Aberdeen on 4 October were, as he reported to Forster on the 10th, 'crammed to the street, twice in one day'. And he began his letter by saying, 'I cannot tell you what the demonstrations of personal regard and respect are', going on to describe 'how common people and gentlefolks will stop me in the street and say: "Mr Dickens, will you let me touch the hand that has filled my home with so many friends?"'

It seems to have been a similar story with regard to his other public appearances this autumn. He was received 'with acclamation' both on 21 July at a meeting for the foundation of a Dramatic College and on 3 December at a public prize-giving in Manchester. On 4 December a banquet in his honour was held at Coventry, where he was presented with a gold watch and one speaker claimed he had '"done more than any other man living" to close the gulf between rich and poor'. What might strike us most today about the report of the occasion is that Dickens, after all the scandalmongering about his private life of the previous six months, should end his acceptance speech by making sexist jokes (as we would now call them) that might seem to have a strong application to his own case. He took his cue for such a peroration from the legendary local heroine, Lady Godiva. 'We know', he said amid 'roars of laughter', 'that *she* was a woman. . . . and we know every day of our lives that the Fates are women.' It is, of course, possible, but I think very unlikely, that he was actually making a joke against himself.

By the time he delivered his Coventry speech, Dickens had, for most of the time since the announcement of his separation from his wife, been living, on an almost daily basis, much more in the public eye than ever before, even in *his* very high-profile career. For three and a half months, from the beginning of August to mid-November, he had been constantly on the road (the *rail*road, that is) with his team, appearing before huge audiences in almost every region of the United Kingdom. His occasional brief breaks were mostly spent at Gad's Hill, his country home in Kent. Ellen, too, was also continuously in the public eye throughout 1858, though in a much less spectacular way. She was working at the Haymarket, London's leading comedy theatre, where she played small parts but still attracted some notice from the theatrical journal *The Era*, which commended her 'pretty face and well-developed figure'. Gossip about Dickens's association with her still continued, as can be seen from a letter written to a friend by Thackeray's daughter Annie, later Lady Ritchie, in late December 1858: 'Papa says the story is that Charley [Dickens's eldest son, aged twenty-one] met his father & Miss Whatsname Whatever the actress out walking on Hampstead Heath'. Interestingly, she added, 'I don't believe a word of the Scandal' – unlike Papa, it would seem.

CHAPTER TWO

1859–1928
Keeping up appearances

During the last ten years of his life Dickens continued to occupy a position of unique prominence in the life of the British nation. During his reading tours tens of thousands flocked to be dazzled and enraptured by his performances, as they did also in America. 'It was as if some good genius had come among us from another world to dispense favours', recalled the devoted Dickensian W. R. Hughes in his contribution to F. G. Kitton's 1890 *Dickens by Pen and Pencil*. During this last decade Dickens published two more best-selling novels, *Great Expectations* and *Our Mutual Friend*, and at the time of his sudden death he was halfway through publishing a third one, *The Mystery of Edwin Drood*. Every week a new number of his journal *All The Year Round* appeared with the words 'Conducted by Charles Dickens' blazoned all over it. Meanwhile, the rapid development and increasing commercial exploitation of the new technology of photography meant that his image became still more widely familiar to the public than a quarter-century of fame had already made it. A particularly fine series of photographs, taken by Robert Mason in 1866, shows Dickens at his country home,

Gad's Hill Place near Rochester, lounging informally in the porch with family members and guests, reading to his daughters in the garden, and so on. Mason presents him, in fact, as the very model of a prosperous country gentleman relaxing at home in the bosom of his family. Notably absent, however, is any figure identifiable as the lady of the house.

Back in February 1859, after the clamour of 1858 had begun to die down, Thackeray visited Catherine Dickens in her new home and wrote afterwards to his mother, 'the row appears to be [about] not the actress, but the sister in law'. He hastens to add there was 'nothing against Miss H' – meaning, evidently, of a sexual nature – 'except that she is the cleverer & better woman of the two, has got the affections of the children & the father'. It is not clear whether the allegation that Georgina had alienated the Dickens children's affections from their mother stemmed from Catherine herself or was inferred by Thackeray. However, the entry made in his diary by Dickens's former publisher Richard Bentley a few days later, and recently discovered by Patrick Leary, suggests the former to have been the case. Bentley wrote:

> Judge told me that Mrs A'Beckett, the widow of the writer and marshal, told Mrs Haliburton and himself that Mrs Dickens had just reason to complain of his conduct to her sister, who had not only behaved badly toward her herself, but had been the means of estranging her children from her. Dickens at Boulogne was frequently out with her.

Bentley then goes on to give a version of the misdirected jewels story that had been reported to Hans Christian Andersen by Jerichau-Baumann the previous summer. It shows that, at least in some quarters, Amy Sedgwick rather than Ellen Ternan was the prime suspect for having caused Dickens's eye to wander and also depicts Catherine in the unlikely role of domestic detective, a real-life version of Mrs Snagsby in *Bleak House* but with, in her case, some justification for her suspicions:

> The immediate cause of the domestic trouble arose from Dickens having presented a brooch or bracelet with his portrait to Miss Sedgwick or some other actress, which brooch was lost. Dickens then went to Storr and Mortimer, the jewellers in Bond Street [the business was now actually called Hunt and Roskell as correctly named in the 1858 *Detroit Free Press* report of this incident – see above, p. 20], to ask them to advertise a reward for its recovery and requested them that if it should be returned to keep it until he called for it. This they unfortunately did not adhere to but being anxious that he should know it was recovered sent it to Dickens's house. The parcel was opened by Mrs Dickens, who, when she took it to Dickens was told by him Oh Yes! This is mine. Mrs Dickens had her suspicions, no doubt, that all was not as it should be, and went with her daughter to the theatre where, on the appearance of the said actress, the brooch or bracelet was seen upon her.

The following year the American diplomat John Bigelow heard another version of this anecdote at Thackeray's dinner-table, a version which shows that Ellen Ternan had by now replaced Amy Sedgwick as chief suspect, and also introduces some rather improbable-sounding domestic violence on Catherine's part. It also suggests that Thackeray may have been taking a rather more critical view of Georgina's role in the affair by this time. Recording the story, Bigelow could not recall the exact name of the actress involved but remembered he was told that it was the scheming Georgina who had given the game away: 'Mrs Dickens's sister, who had always been in love with [Dickens] and was jealous of Miss Teman [*sic*], told Mrs Dickens of the brooch, and she mounted her husband with comb and brush'.

In 1860, when Dickens sold his grand London home Tavistock House to settle permanently at Gad's Hill, a remarkable paragraph did appear in *The New York Post* (23 October) which, far from criticising him for the breakdown of his marriage, contrived to throw all the blame on Catherine, and even to find an innocent role in the business for an unnamed young actress. Gad's Hill Place itself is seen as having been 'the remote cause of all the great novelist's domestic woes' in that Dickens had from his childhood on so loved the country round Rochester, and been so charmed by Gad's Hill in particular because of its associations with Shakespeare's Falstaff, that he had 'registered a vow that if ever he became rich he would build a house there':

> But by the time he had obtained possession of the means of realizing the object near his heart, Mrs Dickens had become so attached to London life that she positively refused to go into the country. It was in vain that Dickens expostulated, entreated, and explained how difficult it was for him to write in London uninterruptedly, exposed as his popularity rendered him to frequent visitors; Mrs Dickens was inflexible. Ultimately, Dickens went to the new country house accompanied by one of his daughters, and for her sake invited his sister-in-law and a meritorious young actress to become inmates of their dwelling. It was not long before this arrangement became a subject of serious uneasiness to Mrs Dickens. The 'green-eyed monster' is said to have possessed her, and thence arose those serious misunderstandings which led to a dissolution of the marriage compact, and the complete severance of Dickens from London life.

This seems a prime example of how gossip can become so distorted, with or without malicious intent, that blame can be transferred from the injurer to the injured. For what we have here is surely a mangled version of a story originating with Catherine's family. According to a long letter written to a Mrs Stark on 30 August 1858 by her maternal aunt Helen Thomson, Catherine had rejected various 'insulting proposals' made to her by Dickens before the separation. One of these had apparently been that Catherine should stay at Gad's Hill whenever Dickens was resident at their London home in Tavistock Square, and in Tavistock Square whenever he was at Gad's Hill.

Then, on 9 June 1865, Dickens was suddenly thrust into the headlines in his private capacity, in a highly sensational and unwelcome manner. He was returning from one of those frequent trips to France which his public would have known about from following his 'Uncommercial Traveller' papers in *All The Year Round*. A South Eastern Railway train, the so-called 'tidal' one that ran from Folkestone to London, was derailed when crossing the little River Beult between Staplehurst and Headcorn in Kent. Some of the plates holding the rails in place had been loosened by workmen who were not expecting any train at that time, their foreman having consulted the wrong timetable. The train broke into two, and eight of the first-class carriages were smashed to pieces as they tumbled down into the stream and marshy ground beneath the bridge. Dickens's carriage, the leading first-class one, stayed on the rails because the coupling linking it to the next carriage snapped. Dickens, having managed to scramble out, was recognised as for some hours he worked tirelessly among the dead and dying, trying to alleviate suffering by giving the injured water, as well as brandy from a flask that he providentially had with him. A woodcut appeared in *The Penny Illustrated Paper* on 24 June depicting him kneeling on the ground and supporting a prostrate young woman with one arm while lifting a hatful of water towards her lips with the other, a picture both accurately reflecting his admirable behaviour at the time and reinforcing the deeply humane image the public had of him.

As far as his friends and the general public knew, Dickens had been travelling alone. A special train from Charing Cross quickly arrived at Staplehurst to collect the walking wounded and those who had not been injured. *The Times* soon had a reporter on the scene, but he, as was reported in the paper on 10 June, had 'the greatest difficulty in collecting anything like accurate information as to the casualties' or in getting all the passengers' names. Many people were understandably reluctant to give this information for fear of alarming their friends and relations. Three lists of passengers' names were published in *The Times* in successive editions, 10–12 June, but none included any that could have been in any way linked to Dickens. Three months later, in a 'Postscript, in lieu of Preface', published with the last part of *Our Mutual Friend*, Dickens described himself as being accompanied by certain of his fictional characters in the form of the manuscript of Part 16 of the novel and tells how he climbed back into the perilously-suspended carriage to rescue them. That he had similarly rescued two real-life women who had been travelling with him did not become known to the public until some years after his death.

Uncannily, he died on the fifth anniversary of the Staplehurst disaster. During the five intervening years he had continued to be widely loved and revered not only as a great writer but also as a great and good, truly Christian, man. The new intellectual weekly *The Saturday Review* might attack his novels on artistic and political grounds, but his status as what we should now call a 'National Treasure' was absolutely unassailable. His sixth son, Henry Fielding Dickens, remembered that walking with his father in the streets of London had been 'a revelation; a royal progress; people of all degrees and classes taking off their hats and greeting him as he passed'. No more was heard in the press about alleged irregularities in his private life, though his 1867–68 reading tour in America did occasion at least one piece of vituperative journalistic disapprobation. On 7 January 1868 an obscure American journal called *The Northern Monthly Magazine* published 'Some Plain Words Concerning Mr Charles Dickens'. After lambasting him, both as a novelist and as a man, for nine pages and condemning his 'effrontery' in returning to the States in pursuit of dollars after all his 'scurrilous abuse' of the country in *American Notes*, the writer concluded (relying, apparently, on some very out-of-date London gossip) by referring back to the events of 1858:

> After having brought up a very large family by a wife respected by all who knew her, he, in her old age [a bit hard, this, on Catherine, who was forty-three at the time], casts her off and lives apart from her, to consort, if the London press is to be believed, with younger and handsomer mates. His name has been associated unpleasantly with that of his own sister-in-law, Miss Hogarth, and with that of Miss Amy Sedgwick, the noted actress.

This *Northern Monthly* attack notwithstanding, Dickens's American tour proved to be a most triumphal (and profitable) progress and culminated in a grand banquet in his honour in New York.

Just over two years after returning home Dickens was dead. Obituary after obituary extolled him as not only a very great artist but also as what *The Sunday Times* called on 12 June 1870 'the dear friend of men, women and children, even as he was the strong warm friend of humanity'. On the Sunday following his funeral in Westminster Abbey, the Dean, Arthur Stanley, preached on Dickens and his vast and beneficent social influence. His voice, said the Dean, had rung 'through the palaces of the great, as well as through the cottages of the poor'. Queen Victoria wrote in her diary: 'He is a very great loss. He had a large loving mind and the strongest sympathy with the poorer classes.' She made no comment, of course, on his domestic history, but the Royal telegram of sympathy was sent to Catherine in Gloucester Crescent.

With the publication of Dickens's will, the name of Ternan re-appeared in the British press in connection with his for the first time since 1859. The very first person named in the document was a 'Miss Ellen Lawless Ternan' (the surname was misprinted by *The Times* as 'Fernan'), who received a bequest of £1,000, the same amount as Dickens left to his daughter Mamie. Given the mood of national mourning for such a beloved figure, only a very foolhardy journalist would have seized on this detail to revive the scandals of twelve years before. Nor was Ternan a name likely to feature in the first biographies and biographical sketches that were rushed out after Dickens's death. Among these was an essay by George Augustus Sala, who had been one of 'Dickens's young men' on *Household Words* and who now wrote for *The Daily Telegraph*. His 140-page *Charles Dickens*, published by Routledge, was a much-expanded version of a piece he had written for the *Telegraph* two days after Dickens's death. Towards the end of it he does allude to the failure of Dickens's marriage, since it would, he wrote, have been 'cowardly dishonesty' to suppress all reference to what he calls 'this great shadow' that fell across Dickens's hearth. He deplores Dickens's decision to publish his 'Personal' statement, since the 'scandalous imputations' it was meant to counteract were 'so wildly improbable in their nature and so obscure that their very existence was ignored by ninety-nine out of every hundred men and women who began to wonder at the passionateness of his defence'. Nothing more needed to be, or could be, said about this subject, Sala declared, but he could not resist dropping a heavy hint that there might well have been some real fire beneath all the smoke: 'Those who have a right to speak have not spoken; and the world has no right to inquire into the mystery – if any mystery there be – nor will have, any time these fifty years.'

The first book-length biography appeared within a fortnight of Dickens's death. This was *Charles Dickens: The Story of His Life*, published and partly written by a freebooting publisher/ bookseller (and later part-time pornographer) called John Camden Hotten in collaboration with a journalist called H. T. Taverner. It was impudently bound so as to be uniform with Chapman and Hall's prestigious 'Charles Dickens Edition' of Dickens's works. The authors touch extremely circumspectly, in fact, upon the events of 1858 and strive to make the marital breakdown appear to have been nobody's fault: 'a misunderstanding had arisen betwixt Mr and Mrs Dickens, of a purely domestic character – so domestic – almost trivial, indeed – that neither law nor friendly arbitration could define or fix the difficulty sufficiently clear to adjudicate upon it'.

Like Sala, Hotten and Taverner deplore Dickens's decision to go public with regard to the separation. His 'Personal' statement, they assert (they make no mention of the 'Violated Letter'), simply stirred up newspaper comment, 'in some cases exceedingly rancorous and spiteful, – and various long letters and documents from friends on both sides appeared in the public journals' (if this was indeed the case, the bulk of these 'letters and documents' has yet to be traced). Hotten apparently submitted proofs of his book to Catherine, asking her to correct any inaccuracies, but we do not know whether she actually read them. Meanwhile, other hastily-compiled biographies appeared both in Britain and in America, but the only one to hint at possible scandal, apart from Sala's, was Robert Shelton Mackenzie's, published in Philadelphia. Mackenzie had known both Dickens and his father during his time as a journalist in London in the 1840s before he emigrated to America. In his *Life of Charles Dickens* he reprinted both the 'Violated Letter' and the 'Personal' statement, finding the latter 'very impressive – by reason of its candor and simplicity' and approving it as a 'mere statement of plain facts, *as* facts'. As to the 'Violated Letter', Mackenzie assumes – or pretends to assume – that the unnamed 'young lady' so ardently referred to in it by Dickens must have been Georgina, to whom, malicious gossips alleged, he 'had been only too much attached'. Mackenzie comments, '*He* could not have written a stronger disclaimer, without doing the lady the great wrong of publishing her name' (the fact that her name is all over the earlier part of this document does not signify, apparently). Georgina as a cause of Dickens's marital difficulties did figure in a rather odd way in F. B. Perkins's reference to the end of the marriage in his *Charles Dickens: A Sketch of his Life and Works*, published by Putnam and Sons in New York in 1870:

It is supposed by some that the appearance of Mrs Dickens's sister, Miss Hogarth, as one of the actors in Mr Collins's play of 'The Light-House' [staged by Dickens at Tavistock House], in 1855, was in some way the cause of vexation to Mrs Dickens, and thus the reason of the open quarrel which resulted in the separation of 1856 [*sic*]. Others suppose this appearance to have been only the occasion of the disagreement in question. ... There is reason to suppose, aside from the weight of Mr Dickens's own solemn assertions, that he and his wife were extremely ill-suited to each other.

Perkins then proceeds to quote the 'Violated Letter' in full but without comment.

In 1871 came the eagerly-awaited first volume of the official biography by John Forster, Dickens's bosom friend and his literary adviser for nearly the whole of his career. This contained such sensational revelations about Dickens's early years (his father's money troubles and period of imprisonment in the Marshalsea, his own period of 'degrading' toil in the blacking factory and street vagrancy, and his enduringly resentful feelings towards his mother) that there was perhaps some expectation of comparably sensational revelations in a later volume about the failure of his marriage. But Georgina had, as she wrote to her great pen-friend Annie Fields, wife of Dickens's American publisher, complete confidence in Forster's discretion. She had, she told Annie, discussed with him the question of how the subject of the marital breakdown should be handled and she felt wholly confident that he would do it in such a way as to give '*no gratification to scandalous curiosity*'. She did, however, regret that since Catherine was still alive, Forster could say nothing about what Georgina calls 'the peculiarities of her character' which, if set against those of Dickens himself, 'would be an explanation for a good deal'. Dickens's eldest daughter, Mamie, also felt absolute confidence in Forster's discretion, as shown in a letter sent to her brother Alfred out in Australia just before Forster's first volume appeared: 'Mr Forster thinks it better to publish it [the biography] at once, with a view to stopping all sorts of lying reports, which of course it clears.'

Georgina and Mamie would have been a good deal less pleased with an article entitled 'Reminiscences of Charles Dickens: from a Young Lady's Diary' that appeared in *The Englishwoman's Domestic Magazine* in 1871 signed with the initials E.E.C. Eleanor Emma Christian, *née* Picken, had been twenty years old and unmarried when she met the thirty-eight-year-old Dickens on holiday with his family at Broadstairs, where she was also holidaying with a family called Smithson who were good friends of the Dickenses. In her 'Reminiscences' she paints a vivid picture of the romping and boisterous manner in which Dickens flirted with her and her friend Milly Thompson, 'a charming woman of a certain age'. Her most sensational reminiscence is of Dickens rushing her down to the end of the pier one evening just as the tide was coming in and holding her there by main force, terrified, until the water was up to their knees and her only silk dress was ruined. Meanwhile he was spouting bombastic nonsense

('Don't struggle, poor little bird: you are powerless in the claws of such a kite as this child!' etc., etc.) until she was in her desperation able to wrestle herself free. Christian published further reminiscences of Dickens in 1888 that did not show him in a particularly amiable light, but both her articles were studiously ignored by reverential collectors of Dickensiana, working under the eye of Georgina Hogarth in the 1890s and early 1900s. They were to come into their own, however, in the 1960s and 1970s when Dickens acquired a 'swinging' media image and Christian was referred to in *The Sunday Times* for 29 March 1970 (trailing Thames Television's *Life of Dickens* to be shown later that year) as having become 'one of the author's mistresses'.

Back in the 1870s, Georgina and Mamie's faith in Forster was certainly vindicated. The third and final volume of his *Life* duly appeared at the beginning of 1874, and chapter 7 covering the years 1857–8 was headed, with studied anti-sensationalism, 'What happened at this time'. Describing the end of the marriage, Forster scrupulously avoids all details, confining himself to a general reference to the 'many sorrowful misunderstandings' that transpired between Dickens and Catherine during this period, a time which, he stresses, was for Dickens one of greatly increased psychological tension and emotional restlessness. Forster quotes from a letter Dickens wrote to him lamenting the basic incompatibility of temperament that he believed to exist as regarded himself and Catherine, 'amiable and complying' though Dickens declared her to be. He quotes also Dickens's identification of himself with his fictional alter ego David Copperfield in respect of the adult David's being haunted in his marriage to Dora by a crushing sense of what he calls the 'one happiness I have missed in life, and one friend and companion I have never made'. Forster is, of course, very careful to give no hint that the end of the Dickens marriage might have been precipitated by the appearance on the scene of anyone who might have seemed ideally suited to fulfil that role for him. Rather, he so strongly links Dickens's restlessness and distress with his intense hankering to embark on a new career as a public reader of his own work (a development much deplored by Forster) that his mention of the actual end of the marriage – 'Thenceforward he and his wife lived apart' – seems to come almost as an afterthought.

Forster ends this eggshell-treading section of his work by recalling his own strenuous opposition to Dickens's issuing of public statements about his private affairs no matter how much provocation he had had from 'miserable gossip'. In its review of Forster's last volume, *The Times* (9 February 1874) agreed with his deprecation of Dickens's decision to publish his 'Personal' statement. The reviewer commented (with scant regard for Catherine's feelings) that Dickens 'was bound, it may be, to a very ordinary wife, and instead of making the best he made the worst of it'. He should have kept silent, not least because of 'other complications and entanglements' (presumably an oblique reference to Georgina, and, conceivably, to Ellen also) that 'went to swell the case against [him], and made it look worse than it actually was'. James Payn, a former contributor to *Household Words*, was, in his *Chambers's Journal* review of Forster's final volume, a good deal more severe on Dickens, whom he otherwise greatly admired. He thought that Dickens's discovery of marital incompatibility came 'rather late in the day' and was not something with which any 'properly constituted mind can sympathise, more particularly when it is known, as we happen to know, that Mrs Dickens is a person of amiable temperament, lady-like in manners, and wholly irreproachable in her life and conversation'. Probably, the majority of readers of Forster's third volume would have concurred with a comment by the reviewer for the New York *International Review*: 'if there are certain passages of Mr Dickens's life suppressed in these volumes, we are relieved from stories of scandals over which the veil had better rest at present, and perhaps for ever'.

The London correspondent of a small-circulation New York paper called *The Arcadian*, someone who seems to have been personally acquainted with Dickens and his circle, evidently felt that a bit of veil-raising might do more good than harm in counteracting scurrility. He filed a column which was copied into a number of other papers like *The Bangor Daily Whig and Courier* (6 August 1874). Reports of a new production of *The Frozen Deep* in Boston, Massachusetts, prompt 'sad reflections' in this correspondent's mind since the original production of this play in Manchester (the date is incorrectly given here as 1859) 'was indirectly the means of bringing about much of Dickens's domestic unhappiness'. One of the professional actresses recruited for this Manchester staging of the play was 'Miss Ellen Ternan', who 'was then a fresh, pleasant-looking girl, not especially pretty, but possessing a good figure and an extremely agreeable manner'. The *Arcadian*'s correspondent continues by way of a reference to Goethe:

> If ever the German poet's doctorine [*sic*] of elective affinities was proved to be true, it was when Dickens and Miss Ternan met. It was evident to nearly all of us that the two were mutually infatuated. Dickens was constantly at her side, though his manner was carefully guarded. Mrs Dickens was with the party, but she did not appear to notice the intimacy. Very soon after these performances Miss Ternan, at Dickens' wish, left the stage. His affection for her was said to have been purely platonic, and I have never met anyone who was disposed to dispute this belief.

The *Arcadian*'s correspondent goes on to say that this platonic friendship nevertheless proved to be the proximate cause of the end of the Dickens marriage (which for many years had been 'anything but happy'). He then relates a version he has heard of the misdirected jewels anecdote. In this, Catherine Dickens was surprised by an assistant at a fashionable West End jeweller's where she was a regular customer asking her how she liked her new bracelet. The discovery that Dickens had recently ordered such an item clearly not intended for herself 'opened her eyes' about his relationship with Ellen 'and a separation speedily followed'.

The Dickens scandal continued cropping up in the American press for many more years. On 27 September 1885 *The Rocky Mountain News* managed, in time-honoured fashion, to get the best of both worlds by retailing scurrilous gossip and, as it were in the same breath, condemning its circulation:

A paragraph has been making the round of the papers explaining the real cause of the separation of Charles Dickens and his wife as follows: "The secret was revealed on the publication of Dickens's will. The first bequest is £1,000 to Miss T – (Ternan), the daughter of a worthy woman and a distinguished actress. It seems that Dickens, who had sent her to Italy for musical education, became enamored of the girl, and she bore him three children. Nothing more need be said."

The New York *World* takes it up and disputes it in toto, and says Miss Fanny Ternan never had any children. She married a Mr Trollope and never received a cent from Mr. Dickens. Dickens gave a £1,000 to her sister Ellen, who married a young clergyman to whom she had long been engaged.

The lack of feeling and innate delicacy which makes these literary ghouls prowl around and make a cent with a sensational story on a corpse is beyond comprehension.

Forster meanwhile made no changes to the text of his discussion of the marital breakdown when he re-issued his *Life* in 1876, the year that he himself died. That the 'stories of scandal' deplored by the writer in the *International Review* still persisted in some circles is testified by a letter written in the same year from the widow of Dickens's poet-friend Bryan Procter (Barry Cornwall) to Nina Lehmann. She tells her of a recent meeting with Tom Trollope and his wife Fanny, Ellen's eldest sister ('Miss Turnan that was'), at a dinner-party given by Anthony Trollope and reports that 'Antony & Tom say it was only *friendship* between Dickens & Miss Turnan –!' Mrs Procter's italics and her exclamation mark speak volumes.

Four years later came a two-volume selection of Dickens's letters edited by Georgina and Mamie. Their preface describes their work as a 'supplement' to Forster's biography (the volumes were bound so as to be uniform with those of the first edition of the *Life*), which as a biography was 'perfect and exhaustive'. The excuse for their edition was that, although 'no man ever expressed *himself* more in his letters than Charles Dickens', Forster's scheme for his book had necessarily excluded virtually all Dickens's letters apart from those written to Forster himself (they do not explain the necessity they invoke). Following editorial procedures that were pretty cavalier even by the standards of the day, Georgina and Mamie altered the texts of various letters, silently omitting anything deemed too personal or likely to give offence, and dovetailing together passages from letters of widely different date. The resulting collection leaves, as the Dickens scholar K. J. Fielding observed, the impression that Dickens was 'a charming eccentric who passed most of his time at the seaside with his family at Broadstairs and Boulogne, or in getting up private theatricals'. Some of Dickens's affectionate earlier letters to Catherine were included (a reconcilement had taken place between Georgina and Catherine following Dickens's death). Catherine was, according to Georgina, very pleased that the letters edition was being undertaken, but she did not live to see it in print. Georgina and Mamie preface each year of Dickens's life with a 'Narrative', a brief – and singularly uninformative – biographical summary of that year. Predictably, there is no mention of Dickens's separation from his wife in the 'Narrative' for 1858.

One passage that, rather surprisingly perhaps, Georgina and Mamie did allow to stand occurs in a letter of 13 June 1865 from Dickens to his old friend and solicitor Thomas Mitton about the Staplehurst disaster. Dickens writes that 'two ladies, an old one and a young one', were sharing his compartment but does not say whether or not they were actually of his party. That he reports the older lady as sitting opposite to him and the younger one as sitting next to him would seem to suggest that they were. He describes to Mitton catching hold of both of them at the moment of the crash, calming them, and helping them to escape from the wreck along with all the other people in that carriage. A third volume of selected letters published by Georgina and Mamie in 1882 included one revealing that Dickens did actually know at least one person in his compartment: 'On that horrible Staplehurst day', he wrote to his friend T. J. Serle on 29 July 1868, 'I had not the slightest idea that I knew any one in the train out of my own compartment'. Georgina and Mamie must have realised pretty quickly that this letter might well get linked by the curious with the letter to Mitton about the two ladies who had been in his compartment and they proceeded to excise from the second edition (of all three volumes of their selected letters) published later in 1882 both this passage *and* the earlier one about the two ladies. Although no curiosity seems to have been aroused in the readers of these best-selling volumes as to just who these female fellow-passengers might have been, Georgina and Mamie evidently wanted to take no chances.

Reviews of successive volumes of this family-edited collection of Dickens letters were generally positive but convey no sense of new things about Dickens being revealed through them. In the main, reviewers were simply confirmed in their belief that Dickens was a great and good man, though perhaps neither a very deep-thinking nor an emotionally complex one. William Brighty Rands concluded (pseudonymously) in *The Contemporary Review* for January 1880, piquantly enough in view of later developments, that Dickens's letters showed him to have been a man who 'had but little secretiveness'. Georgina and Mamie's volumes were followed in 1892 by Laurence Hutton's careful edition of a selection made by Georgina from Dickens's letters to Wilkie Collins. Collins, whose own private life, involving as it did not one but two non-marital establishments, was decidedly on the unconventional side, had helped Georgina and Mamie with the earlier compilations. He had died in 1889, taking with him to the grave whatever he knew about the Dickens–Ellen relationship as well as his memories of the sprees Dickens and he had enjoyed together in Paris, excursions that have been the subject of much excited speculation by later commentators. Then in 1912, the centenary year of Dickens's birth, a volume appeared with the title *Charles Dickens as Editor*. This was a selection of letters written to W. H. Wills, sub-editor of Dickens's weekly magazines and for nearly twenty years his confidential man of business. These letters had been selected and edited (just how discreetly edited would not appear for forty years) by Wills's great-nephew Rudolph Lehmann, who wrote a preface focusing on the way they confirm many already-known admirable traits of Dickens's character – his indefatigable attention to business, for example, and how he was 'always devoted to good causes and perfectly fearless in his efforts to promote them'.

By 1912 Dickens's apotheosis in the English-speaking world was well under way, with Georgina Hogarth, who was to die in her ninetieth year in 1917, as chief priestess of his cult. 'No one living has so wide and intimate a knowledge of Charles Dickens, or exercises a more loving guardianship of his memory', declared the American journal *Nash's Magazine* when publishing Georgina's portrait in 1911. This guardianship, it later transpired, involved remaining, along with Mamie, on terms of warm friendship with Ellen, now married to the highly respectable Margate headmaster George Wharton Robinson, by whom she had had two children. Adolphus Ward gratefully acknowledges Georgina's help in his writing of his 1882 life of Dickens for Macmillan's prestigious 'English Men of Letters' series, so we may presume he received her imprimatur for saying, with studied vagueness, that the reasons for Dickens's separation from his wife had been 'an open secret to his friends and acquaintances', also that nothing in Dickens's surviving letters to Catherine suggests that he ever loved her 'with that affection before which so-called incompatibilities of habits, temper, or disposition fade into nothingness'. We may note, too, that Ward goes out of his way to pay tribute to 'the self-sacrificing and devoted care' Georgina gave to the younger Dickens children. Clearly, the implication here is that Catherine had indeed been the inadequate mother depicted in the 'Violated Letter'.

Fortunately, Henry, Dickens's lawyer son, was able to shield Georgina from all knowledge of a preposterous fraud attempted in Calcutta in 1908 whereby a charity was being solicited for money on behalf of a child alleged to be her grandson, offspring of a son she had borne Dickens in 1854. This self-proclaimed son, who called himself Hector Charles Bulwer Lytton Dickens but whose real name was Charley Peters, claimed that he had been brought to Gad's Hill at the age of three and this had caused an outraged Catherine, on discovering his parentage, to leave her home for ever. He further claimed that Dickens had never got round to fulfilling his expressed intention of marrying Georgina (something that he could not, of course, have done legally) and that when he died both she and her child (i.e., Charley himself) were turned out of Gad's Hill by the rest of the family. He had eventually settled, so his story went, in Australia, where he met up again with Alfred and Edward Dickens whom he claimed as half-brothers and who, so he asserted, had accepted the relationship. Now living in Calcutta, he needed money to support his own child, hence his application to the charity, an application supported by letters from various Australian notables who all believed that he was the scandalously badly treated natural son of Dickens. Henry told B. W. Matz, the then Honorary Editor of *The Dickensian*, that it made his blood boil 'to think my dear revered old aunt should be made the subject of such a scandalous story' and he lost no time in sending a denial and supporting evidence to Calcutta. Claire Tomalin, working on her biography of Ellen in the 1980s, came across this ludicrous story still going strong, and it resurfaced in quite a spectacular manner as recently as 2011. An engraved diamond ring alleged to have been given by Tennyson to Alfred Dickens, who was named after him, and subsequently by Alfred in Australia to his 'half-brother' Hector Dickens, alias Charley Peters, was sold in a provincial English auction house for £64,000.

Georgina's guardianship of the 'beloved memory' notwithstanding, it would seem that rumours about her part in the failure of Dickens's marriage, other than Charley Peters's fantastic yarn, did persist into the twentieth century, as we gather from Walter Dexter's history of the Dickens Fellowship published in the Fellowship's journal *The Dickensian* in 1944. In this he recalls how surprised he had been, back in 1905, at seeing Georgina fêted as a guest of honour at the Fellowship's first Dickens Birthday Dinner, because 'in common with many people of the time, I was under the impression that it was she who was the cause of the estrangement between Dickens and his wife!' He was, however, soon put right about this by other Fellowship members.

In his retrospective piece Dexter studiously avoids any mention of Ellen Ternan. The period about which he was writing was one in which her name certainly seemed to vanish from the record apart from one curious reference to her in 1910. In the 'Introduction' to his *Dickens and the Drama* published in that year S. J. Adair Fitzgerald mentions a one-act play, apparently written in Melbourne in 1895 by one John Garraway and set behind the scenes of one of the Manchester performances of *The Frozen Deep* in 1857. Before dismissing this 'precious comedy' as utterly insignificant, Fitzgerald mentions that it introduces 'Miss Ternan' who 'played in several pieces with Dickens' and notes that 'round this actress and Dickens is woven a slight love affair'. Whether or not Garraway had had contact with either of Dickens's sons then in Australia (both of them at times living in Melbourne) we do not know, any more than we know how much they themselves would have known or surmised about Ellen and her relations with their father. Alfred had left England in 1865 aged twenty, with sixteen-year-old Edward following him to Australia three years later.

Meanwhile, in 1908 another woman, from further back in Dickens's past than 1858, was revealed when the Boston Bibliophile Society published *Charles Dickens and Maria Beadnell: Private Correspondence*. This volume presented a series of extraordinary letters written by Dickens to Maria Beadnell, the pretty banker's daughter whom he had passionately but unavailingly adored between the ages of eighteen and twenty-one. The earlier letters dated from the 1830s, but there was also a remarkable sequence of three long epistles written in early 1855, after Maria, now Mrs Henry Winter, had suddenly re-established contact with Dickens by letter. They were written in the short interval before he could meet her and be abruptly disillusioned by her changed appearance. They are impassioned letters recalling his love for her in astonishing detail and seeming at one point to be proposing that they should embark on some kind of *amitié amoureuse* establishing 'a confidence between us which still once more, in perfect innocence and good faith, may be between ourselves alone'. Maria must have made some comparable sort of counter-suggestion as

Dickens went on to say: 'All that you propose I accept with my whole heart. Whom can you ever trust if it be not your old lover?'

These are certainly remarkable words for a middle-aged married man and father of ten to be writing to an old flame who is now herself married to someone else, and they throw a strange light on Dickens's emotional state in early 1855. Georgina, aware as she was of the part Maria had played in Dickens's life, must have believed that his letters to her contained matter which should remain private, and she and Henry were able, as the undoubted owners of the copyright in Dickens's letters, to arrange for a ban to be placed on the importation into the UK of any copies of this volume. Matz did manage to see a copy, however, and evidently agreed with the claim made in the preface that 'the correspondence contains nothing which need shock the most sensitive morals . . . nothing that could militate against [Dickens's] reputation or minimise the reverence in which his memory is held'. He tried to get Georgina to change her mind, but after reading the letters she remained, unsurprisingly, resolutely opposed to their publication in England. In 1882 she herself had, in fact, included one later, anodyne, letter to Maria in the third volume of her and Mamie's edition of Dickens's letters with a note that Maria had been 'a very dear friend and companion of Charles Dickens in his youth' and that was all she wanted the public to know about her. After Maria's death Matz did manage to persuade Sir Henry to allow these letters to be published in the *Strand Magazine* with some commentary by Matz himself, but at the last moment Sir Henry insisted on substituting rows of asterisks for various phrases in the letters, which of course merely aroused suspicions that scandalous material was being suppressed. Eventually, Walter Dexter, Matz's successor as editor of *The Dickensian*, armed with a unanimous resolution from the Fellowship's Executive Committee urging the publication in full of the Beadnell letters 'to protect Dickens's good name', did get Sir Henry grudgingly to sanction this. Meanwhile, J. W. T. Ley, a former Hon. General Secretary of the Dickens Fellowship, had included lengthy notes on Maria and Dickens's youthful passion for her in his new annotated edition of Forster's life published in June 1928. In his note 69 he tells the whole story of the affair and in note 448, on the separation, he argues that Dickens's disillusionment with Maria when he saw her again contributed towards making his marriage no longer tolerable for him.

Sir Henry was reported in the *Daily Express* of 28 April 1928 as saying that he knew nothing about Ley's edition of Forster and had no wish to do so, and it is significant that the names in Ley's acknowledgements do not include that of a single member of the Dickens family but are confined to Matz, Dexter, Kitton and other Fellowship worthies. When Dexter again raised with Sir Henry the subject of the publication of Dickens's letters to Maria Beadnell he was sharply rebuffed and it was not until the following year, after Sir Henry had died, that he was finally able to produce a British edition of them.

The years between 1870 and 1928 saw an ever-increasing flood of topographical, bibliographical and biographical studies devoted to Dickens and his work by his admirers. An appreciable number of these were written by the indefatigable Frederic G. Kitton. In his Foreword to his *Charles Dickens by Pen and Pencil* (1889–90) he records his 'warmest thanks' to Georgina for 'much valued advice' and for 'her kindness in looking over the "proofs" during their progress through the press'. He does not seem to have consulted her about the material included in the Supplement he published in 1890, perhaps thinking the inclusion of a long adoring memoir of her father by Mamie was a sufficient guarantee of its acceptability. Georgina, however, complained bitterly to the publishers that Kitton had been 'too ready to accept contributions from *everybody*! Whether they really knew anything of

Mr Dickens – or whether they did *not*!' and reminded them that she had stopped a great deal of material that was '*absolutely untrue*' from appearing in the original volume. No comment by her seems to have survived regarding Kitton's earlier compilation, *Dickensiana: A Bibliography of the Literature relating to Charles Dickens and His Writings*, which was brought out by a different publisher in 1886 and dedicated to Charles Dickens Junior. It is certainly hard to imagine that she or the dedicatee or any member of the Dickens family, if they *had* seen the proofs of this book, would have passed the reprinting in it of the paragraph from the 1860 *New York Post* quoted above (p. 30) with its mention of 'a meritorious young actress' going to live at Gad's Hill as a companion for Mamie. It may have been Kitton's indiscriminate hoovering up of everything to do with Dickens that caused Kate Perugini to describe him to George Bernard Shaw in a letter now in the British Library as 'weak and credulous' – and even to confess to a guilty wish that he 'had been drowned at birth'.

Kitton's life-span was rather longer than Kate might have wished, but he died at a comparatively young age in 1904 – not, however, before he had played a leading role in the founding of the Dickens Fellowship and the planning of its journal *The Dickensian* of which he was to have been the first editor. The original stated aims of the Fellowship (and it is, of course, significant that the name chosen was 'Fellowship' rather than 'Society') reflect Dickens's unique status at this time among broad swathes of the British and American reading public. The second and third of the four aims as originally formulated were as follows :

To spread the love of humanity, which is the keynote of all [Dickens's] work;

To take such measures as may be deemed expedient to remedy those existing social evils, the amelioration of which would have

appealed so strongly to the heart of Charles Dickens, and to help
in every possible direction in the cause of the poor and oppressed.

In its activities the Fellowship intermingled meat-teas for poor
children and sewing-bees to make clothing for the poor with
topographical investigations, speculations about the intended
ending of *Edwin Drood*, and lectures on Dickens's life and
works. The organisation flourished and soon had branches in
many parts of the United Kingdom and elsewhere in the
English-speaking world, remarkable testimony to Dickens's
unique status as a great humanitarian hero in the late nineteenth
and early twentieth centuries.

Kitton was not the only researcher into her father's life about
whom Kate Perugini felt nervous. There was also, she wrote to
Shaw in 1893, 'a wretch called Wright' who was, as she put it,
'sniffing around'. She was referring to Thomas Wright who had
published a life of the poet William Cowper in 1892. In his
posthumously-published *Autobiography* Wright describes himself
as having always had a special interest 'in the love experiences,
regular or irregular, of men of genius'. He was also one of the
pioneers of a new sort of less respectful, more investigative, kind
of biography and, having Dickens in his sights, he began corre-
sponding with people like the former *All The Year Round*
contributor John Hollingshead who could provide him with
first-hand information about his subject. Sala soon got wind of
his activities and launched a pre-emptive strike in *The Manchester
Evening News* for 16 September 1893, where he repeated
his 1870 assertion that there were circumstances connected
with Dickens's later life that ought not to be made public for
'fifty years to come at the very least'. (In 1870, we remember, he
had only said that there *might* be such circumstances, now he
states unequivocally that they did exist.) Georgina, too, wrote
privately, and according to Wright himself, 'furiously', to him on

21 October demanding that he abandon his project. Kate, however, whose attitude to her adored 'uncanny genius' of a father was, as was to become publicly clear some forty years later, rather more complex than her aunt's or Mamie's, took a more conciliatory line. She 'showed herself reasonable', Wright recalled, 'and expressed herself very kindly by letter'. He began publishing what he called 'Foundations for a Life of Charles Dickens' in *The Chatham and Rochester News* on 22 January 1898, a series which continued in irregular instalments until 22 April 1899. A note states: 'The author invites criticism for he hopes to make the work, before it appears in book form, practically exhaustive. Letters should be sent to the author.' Ellen gets only a passing mention as 'Miss Ellen Lawless Ternan – the lady to whom he left by will "the sum of £1,000"'. In the event Wright had, it seems, to put his Dickens project aside because of difficulties with his publisher and nearly forty years were to pass before it saw the light of day.

Meanwhile, a piece of book-making by the wife of the editor of a fashionable newspaper had given a fairly broad hint about those delicate 'circumstances' concerning which Sala dropped such portentous hints:

Charles Dickens was once by chance my fellow-traveller on the Boulogne packet: travelling with him was a lady not his wife, nor his sister-in-law, yet he strutted about the deck with the air of a man bristling with self-importance, every line of his face and every gesture of his limbs seemed haughtily to say – 'Look at me; make the most of your chance. I am the great, the *only* Charles Dickens: whatever I may choose to do is justified by that fact.'. . . As a rule, the private life of a public man ought perhaps to be protected from the curiosity of the world; but when he has had the bad taste to parade the unwarrantable acts of his private life so as to give public scandal, his conduct

> cannot escape criticism. . . . None who know the history of [Catherine Dickens's] outraged life, can respect Dickens as a man, however much they may admire him as a writer.

The author of this feline paragraph was Julia Clare Byrne, wife of the editor of *The Morning Post*, very much the top people's paper of the day, and the book was her *Gossip of the Century*, published in 1892. The *Post* had generally been hostile to Dickens, but it is still somewhat surprising that Clare Byrne should have been so explicit. Georgina and the Dickens family, if they were aware of the passage, prudently chose to ignore it.

Another hinter at impropriety was the redoubtable journalist and novelist Eliza Lynn Linton, who had been a regular contributor to Dickens's *All The Year Round*. In her *My Literary Life*, posthumously published in 1899, she claimed to have been given confidential information about the private lives of both Dickens and Thackeray. 'Both men', she wrote, 'could, and did, love deeply, passionately, madly, and the secret history of their lives has yet to be written'. Still more thrillingly, she states that Dickens was made the dupe of 'one cleverer, more astute, less straight than himself, who sailed round him and deceived him from start to finish'. This might well refer to Ellen since, as Claire Tomalin observes, 'It's hard to think who else she could have meant'.

Many reminiscences of Dickens by his children appeared during the forty years following his death, all building up an image of him as a wonderful, kind and loving father, a splendid and generous host, the life and soul of social occasions, a phenomenally hard worker, a great and good man. Mamie Dickens's *My Father As I Recall Him* (1896) stands out here, as also does Kate Perugini's moving account in *The Pall Mall Gazette* for June 1906 ('Edwin Drood and the Last Days of Dickens') of her last time together with her father a few days before his death, an account which was to resurface, with some rather startling additions, over thirty years later. She also worked on a full-scale biography of her father, perhaps stirred thereto by fear of what Wright might discover and publish, but drew back from publishing it because she disliked the idea of what she called in a letter to the *Punch* historian M. H. Spielmann published in *The Dickensian* in 1980 '"giving away" my father and mother for pounds shillings and pence'. The only reason that would make her change her mind, she told Spielmann, who was advising her on the project, 'would be any flagrant attack upon my father's character'. She perhaps had her eye on Wright when she wrote this.

Moving as she very much did in the literary and artistic world of late Victorian and Edwardian England, Kate Perugini may have been more aware than the rest of her family, or than most members of the Dickens Fellowship, that she was living through a period that was witnessing great and strongly contested changes in the art and practice of biography dating back at least to James Anthony Froude's authorised life of his friend Carlyle (1882–84). This had shocked the great man's disciples and admirers by revealing how much misery his wife had endured and how stricken with intense remorse and guilt he had been after her death. The question of how frank and open a biographer could or should be about such matters as his or her subject's personal relationships, especially those that were of a sexual nature, was much debated, and the kind of 'sniffing around' that Wright went in for was a novel, and in some quarters much disapproved of, procedure. Lytton Strachey's *Eminent Victorians*, which appeared in 1918, was certainly not based on investigative interviews, but its lethally witty exposure of some of the less admirable traits of certain great Victorian figures is usually regarded as having put paid to the kind of monumental biography that Wright and his kind were undermining in a different way. Dickens as Great Victorian *par excellence* might have seemed an obvious target for such iconoclasm, but he had, as we have seen, active and effective defenders in Georgina Hogarth and Sir Henry Dickens, as well as in the Dickens Fellowship, and a whole decade was to pass following the publication of *Eminent Victorians* before any mud was publicly thrown at Dickens's spotless image and even then it would be in the form of fiction rather than of biography.

CHAPTER THREE

———

1928–1930
Coming to the boil

The publishing firm of Mills and Boon (Harlequin Mills & Boon since 1971) has been famous since the 1930s for its 'bodice-ripping' romantic fiction, but in all that time it has surely never produced a novel that has proved quite as sensational as one that it published on 7 September 1928. The book was called *This Side Idolatry* and its author was a thirty-four-year-old *Daily Express* journalist named Carl Eric Bechhofer Roberts. Beneath his name on the spine and title-page of the book appeared also the pen-name 'Ephesian' that he had already used in the two previous years for his biographies of two leading Tories, Lord Birkenhead, the former Lord Chancellor (who, incidentally, formally opened the Dickens House Museum, established by the Dickens Fellowship at 48 Doughty Street in 1925), and Winston Churchill. Roberts presumably derived the name from the Biblical narrative of St Paul in Ephesus and he used it to suggest a worshipper. His use of it for this novel based on Dickens's life has, in conjunction with his title, a somewhat ominous ring.

Roberts later claimed in a lengthy 'Foreword' to a reprint of *This Side Idolatry* issued in 1946 that his intention when he began work on Dickens in 1924 had been to write a biography in the usual form. Some first-fruits of his researches had already appeared in the Dickens Fellowship's magazine *The Dickensian* in 1927 in an article detailing some innocuous new discoveries about Dickens's godfather Christopher Huffam. But in the course of their work Roberts and his collaborator Tom Darlow found themselves discovering material about Dickens's life that did not seem at all innocuous. Specifically, they were shocked by Dickens's exploitation of his parents for comic effect in his novels, by his guying of the middle-aged Maria Winter in *Little Dorrit*, and by his treatment of Catherine in the 'Violated Letter'. They were disturbed also by what often seemed very like sharp practice in his treatment of his publishers, and by an incident that Dickens describes twice in his weekly journals in which this supposedly warm-hearted and charitable man insisted on a young girl's being sent to prison merely for the offence of swearing in public. They had also, evidently, got wind of the importance of Ellen Ternan in his later life, though only, it seems, as the proximate cause of the breakdown of his marriage.

Bechhofer Roberts claimed that he was forced to cast the projected biography in the form of a novel owing to the refusal of the Dickens family (presumably Sir Henry) to allow him to quote from unpublished letters – primarily, no doubt, those written by Dickens to Maria Beadnell, the full texts of which had still not been published in Britain. The novel makes dismal reading. Bechhofer Roberts sticks closely to the facts of Dickens's biography as derived from Forster and expends much laboured ingenuity in depicting John Dickens as a real-life Micawber and Elizabeth Dickens as a real-life Mrs Nickleby. He also gives full play to the two Beadnell episodes, the youthful Dickens's romantic infatuation with the young Maria and the mature Dickens's disillusionment with the middle-aged Mrs Winter, as well as to Dickens's seaside horseplay with

Eleanor Picken and her friend. His newly-wed Dickens is soon comparing his young wife unfavourably with her younger sister Mary, and becoming more and more impatient with her as she shows increasing unease about the less admirable aspects of his character and behaviour – his cavalier treatment of his publishers, for example. Bechhofer Roberts's Dickens, intoxicated by his great success, becomes increasingly extravagant in both speech and behaviour, affecting in particular a Sam Wellerish style of talking. Riven by self-pity, he also becomes more and more of a domestic tyrant. It is not long before Catherine, always referred to as Kate, is giving him scrutinising glances 'in which sorrow, contempt and affection mingled'. Georgina, when she comes into the story, is all admiration and compliance, 'tittering' dutifully at her adored brother-in-law's facetiousness, and so on. Unless he had a source we are unaware of, Bechhofer Roberts seems to move into pure invention in his last chapter when he depicts Dickens's first meeting with seventeen-year-old Ellen Ternan. This takes place behind the scenes at the 1857 Haymarket Theatre production of *Atalanta*, a burlesque version of a classical myth, in which Ellen played Prince Hippomenes. Roberts describes her as weeping with shame and embarrassment because she has to appear in revealing tights (surely a somewhat improbable reaction in one who had been on the professional stage since early childhood?). She is comforted, however, by Dickens's assurance that 'a young person so well-made and modest' as she 'had nothing to be ashamed of'. 'What a lovely child!' he says immediately afterwards to his friend and companion Mark Lemon, the Editor of *Punch*, 'and as pure, I swear, as she is beautiful!' He then snubs Lemon for his lip-smacking comment, 'I've seldom seen a more voluptuous figure'. Dickens's subsequent infatuation with Ellen proves to be the last straw for long-suffering Catherine: 'Do you imagine I don't know that you invent every possible excuse to go and see Ellen Ternan?' she demands before she finally bids him go to his 'painted actress' as she can now see no alternative to leaving him: 'I know you through and through,' she tells him, 'and I despise you.'

Bechhofer Roberts ended his novel at this point, merely adding a few brief paragraphs about the separation, Catherine's subsequent dignified silence and continuing love for Dickens, and the bequests in Dickens's will. This is followed by a 'Note' in which Dickens is subjected to some Freudian analysis. Bechhofer Roberts postulates that he suffered from 'mother-fixation' whereby 'unconscious childhood adoration' of his mother produced 'as its conscious effect, a revulsion from her' (so much for the blacking factory!), together with the 'corollary' that he had a strong tendency to idealise women he could not have, like Mary Hogarth. Bechhofer Roberts's implication seems to be that Ellen did *not*, in fact, become Dickens's mistress but succeeded Mary in the role of 'unattainable woman' in his life that was psychologically necessary to him.

Looking back from the vantage point of 1946, when *This Side Idolatry* was reissued, Roberts felt able to write of the original reception of his novel, with pardonable exaggeration:

Never I imagine – certainly not in our lifetime – has any other book created such a public storm. Had it preached cannibalism or unnatural vice as a desirable social reform, my book could not have been attacked so vociferously, so extravagantly or so incorrectly.

On publication day, Friday 7 September 1928, *The Daily Mail* carried a headline 'Was Dickens a Hypocrite? Book that will cause a storm'. It headed a three-column article which summarised the novel's plot and highlighted Dickens's 'monstrous egotism' and his passionate love for Mary Hogarth. The writer does note, however, that the novel 'imputes no guilt to Ellen

Ternan'. *The Yorkshire Evening Press* of the same date reported, under the headline 'Dickens Sensation', that 'a storm of controversy' has been aroused by this novel showing Dickens as 'a philanderer [which it does not] and a selfish egotist [which it certainly does] who did not scruple to caricature intimate friends in his books'. The paper also quoted Bechhofer Roberts as saying that he had been informed, 'by Dickens's relatives', that if he dared to quote the letters to Maria Beadnell that had been privately published in America, 'action would be taken' under copyright law. He had therefore been obliged to use this information in dialogue form. The next day the paper of which Dickens himself had been the first editor, *The Daily News*, featured, in a column headed 'The Honour of "Boz"', an interview with Sir Henry Dickens in which Sir Henry remarked, 'Had this novel appeared in the seventies I can imagine the younger Dickenses looking round for a horsewhip'. He was, he said, not surprised that Bechhofer Roberts was refused access to Dickens's letters and private papers: 'it is not everybody who is assisted to compile biographies'. Noting that 'few are left to challenge' Bechhofer Roberts, Sir Henry states, 'I am preparing a letter to the Press in which I shall go into all the facts very closely' and adds, 'This may take a few days'. In the *Sunday Dispatch* for 9 September, under the headline 'Dickens "Secret Love" Challenge. Author and "Ban on Facts" Offer to Son. Letter to Maria Beadnell', Bechhofer Roberts challenged Sir Henry to remove his ban on the publication in full of the Beadnell letters. 'Does he imagine', he asks, 'that his father's life can always be presented in the form which best suits the prejudices of the family?' 'It is not', he adds with some acerbity, 'as if they were reticent about him'.

Sir Henry seems to have thrown in the sponge almost at once. On 10 September *The Daily News*, after noting that Bechhofer Roberts's 'attack' on Dickens had been 'discussed throughout the country this weekend' causing 'considerable astonishment among the hosts of Dickens-lovers', goes on to quote Sir Henry as describing *This Side Idolatry* as 'utterly unworthy of the slightest consideration' and declining 'to serve the author's purpose by adding to its publicity'. And Bechhofer Roberts had the last word in a letter published in *The Daily Mail* seven days later. He explained why, 'after long enquiry and research', he found himself unable to accept the prevalent 'idolatrous' view of Dickens who, among other reprehensible activities, 'sought a clandestine meeting with an old flame years after their marriages and, finding her old and ugly, pilloried her in his next novel as an amorous, drunken harridan' (a description admirers of the many-splendoured garrulity of good-hearted Flora Finching in *Little Dorrit* might find it hard to accept). The Dickens family, Roberts claimed, knew all about this and other 'defects of his character' but 'deliberately chloroformed the issue by refusing to permit the publication of the letters which establish them'.

The Dickensian meanwhile happily reprinted in its winter number for 1928–29 a string of extracts from over sixteen negative press notices of *This Side Idolatry*, including reviews written by G. K. Chesterton for *The Illustrated London News*, by J. B. Priestley for *The Saturday Review*, and by Leonard Woolf for *The Nation and Athenaeum*. These were followed by more than twenty extracts from equally unfavourable leading articles, and similar editorial comment, from other journals including *The Daily Telegraph*, *The Morning Post* and *Punch*. The last-named magazine gravely warned 'Ephesian' that it was 'no laurel for a young writer to find delight in . . . diminishing the stature of one of the noblest and most generous of his predecessors in the art and craft of letters'. No wonder Mills and Boon felt emboldened to advertise Bechhofer Roberts's book in *The Times* on 18 September as 'The Most Discussed Novel of the Century', proudly displaying this endorsement from the great

American realist novelist Sinclair Lewis: 'This is a book that stirs me – sometimes to anger, but always to feeling that here is that elusive truth whose quest is the one high goal of life'. Lewis was apparently also quoted on the novel's dust-cover, to the disgust of *The Sphere* (quoted in *The Dickensian*'s round-up), as commending Bechhofer Roberts for his 'profound labour' and 'years of hard research'. Beneath Lewis's endorsement in Mills and Boon's advertisement ran the challenging legend, in bold italic type, 'Read this book before criticising it!'

While Bechhofer Roberts was writing his novel, another, older and more established writer had been at work on a biographical study of Dickens and this duly appeared within a few days of Bechhofer Roberts's book. It was called *Dickens: A Portrait in Pencil*, published by Victor Gollancz and written by Ralph Straus, an old-style 'bookman' and member of a bibliophile club called 'Ye Sette of Odd Volumes'. According to Bechhofer Roberts writing in 1946, Gollancz had sent out advance notices to the press promising that Straus's book would contain 'all sorts of sensational revelations about Dickens's life and character', but then had radically to change the tune of his advertising as a result of the sensation caused by *This Side Idolatry*. It does, however, seem on the face of it very unlikely that Straus's book can ever have been advertised in this sensational way, given his connection with Chapman and Hall (he was on the firm's board of directors and his book is dedicated, in fulsome terms, to the chairman Arthur Waugh, one of the founding fathers of the Dickens Fellowship). On the contrary, it benefited from the contrast of its 'gentlemanly' approach to its subject compared with what was seen by J. C. Squire, editor of *John O'London's Weekly*, as Bechhofer Roberts's 'caddishness' which Squire, like Sir Henry, thought deserved the horse-whip. 'Mr Straus', commented *Punch* on 26 September, 'may modestly call his book *A Portrait in Pencil*, but he offers no food to the gutter-perchers'. In his 'Foreword' Straus declared, 'There are incidents in Dickens's life which even now need not be told' and then hastens to add this 'does not mean that Dickens himself was ever guilty of any action whatsoever which could not be told in detail to-day'. He also stated that he had read 'a great number of unpublished family letters from which I have not thought fit to quote', though he had felt free to use any information contained in them that might throw light on Dickens's character. He evidently felt free to quote from those sensitive Dickens letters to Maria Beadnell and must, presumably, have come to an understanding about this with Sir Henry.

Straus also deals very sympathetically with Dickens in the matter of the 'Violated Letter', blaming Arthur Smith for showing it to 'strangers', though he does condemn the publication of the 'Personal' statement ('the stupidest thing [Dickens] ever did in his life'). After alluding to the gossip about Georgina at the time of the separation, Straus identifies 'the young lady' mentioned in 'Personal' as 'a Miss Ellen Lawless Ternan', incorrectly describing her as 'the daughter of a Manchester theatre-manager'. He then quickly adds, 'Of this young lady I shall have very little to say'. Gentleman that he was, all that he did have to say, in fact, was that she, her mother and one of her sisters acted 'more than once' with Dickens, that another sister married a brother of Anthony Trollope, that Ellen herself became 'a very great friend of Dickens's', and that her name stands first in his will, though Straus rather blatantly declines to speculate on possible reasons for this.

This Side Idolatry and Straus's biographical 'portrait in pencil' were reviewed together in a leading article in *The Times Literary Supplement* of 27 September. The article, titled 'Sketches of Boz', was the work of the paper's young assistant editor, D. L. Murray, who blamed Forster's deliberate vagueness about the details of the end of Dickens's marriage for 'the growth of those scandalous stories to which neither an impartial biographer of to-day, Mr Ralph Straus, nor Forster's latest, laborious editor, Mr J. W. T. Ley, gives credit'. Murray deems *This Side Idolatry* both 'unconvincing and an offence against taste' but praises Straus's 'brisk pages', especially for the emphasis placed on the Beadnell affair which left 'a permanent scar on Dickens's soul'. He deplores those 'vulgar judgments' (Bechhofer Roberts's, not Straus's, that is) that crudely misinterpret the nature of Dickens's adoration of Mary Hogarth but contrives to avoid any reference to Ellen Ternan, even though she is mentioned in both the books he is reviewing.

The Ternan relationship is, however, very much alluded to in what is by far the most startling and intriguing of all the press responses to *This Side Idolatry* that I have seen. This was a review written by the veteran Irish journalist and politician T. P. O'Connor. 'Tay Pay', as he was affectionately known, was a close friend of, and regular visitor to, Kate Perugini, now in her ninetieth year. Reviewing *This Side Idolatry* in his own *T.P.'s Weekly* on 29 September, O'Connor deplores the speeches Bechhofer Roberts puts into Catherine Dickens's mouth. They are 'in violent contradiction with her entire attitude in this most unfortunate tragic conflict between her and her husband', as she had, in real life, been always 'dignified, gentle, reticent'. This paragraph, which surely derives from O'Connor's fireside chats with Mrs Perugini, was happily included in *The Dickensian*'s round-up of negative notices. There was, however, no way in which the journal's editor, Walter Dexter, would or could have reprinted O'Connor's next paragraph, boldly headed 'Ellen Ternan' and presumably derived from the same source:

Of course Dickens sinned, and very few men of genius have not sinned in the same way. Unhappy at home, he sought relief abroad. The story of Ellen Ternan may one day be told;

but who today would form a scathing and foul indictment of
any of our contemporary writers because there entered into
their unhappy lives some other woman who gave them
compensation and comfort. There is nothing very remarkable
in the story . . . .

To us today it must seem quite astounding that no other paper
picked up on this explosive paragraph and that Bechhofer
Roberts himself never made any allusion to it. It was to remain
unremarked on, in fact, until Professor Ada Nisbet retrieved it
for her *Dickens and Ellen Ternan* in 1952.

This Side Idolatry seems to have been a great success on both
sides of the Atlantic, so that Mills and Boon were able to adorn
their new advertisement for the book ('Third large British
edition in press. Third large American edition in press') in *The
Times* on 9 October with a dozen admiring quotations from
various American and Canadian newspapers and authors. It was
in America, too, that there was published in this year a book of
reminiscences that fed continuing gossip about Dickens and
Ellen even though it did not name her. Called *Keeping Off The
Shelf*, it was written by an English-born actress, Blanche Whiffen,
now in her eighties, who with her husband Tom, also English by
birth, had made a very successful career in the States. Included
in her book was some ancient tittle-tattle about Dickens and the
end of his marriage, including the tale of the misdirected jewels
that many years later she had gleaned from Tom. He had once
been a choirboy at Rochester Cathedral and had, he had told
her, got to know Dickens 'very well':

> Of course there was a great deal of gossip among his neigh-
> bours about Dickens' family trouble, and it was pretty gener-
> ally conceded that Mrs Dickens was needlessly jealous. Tom
> often told me that Dickens's god-daughter was one of the

causes of jealousy. The young lady was with the novelist a great deal, and was in his company in the railway accident when the coach in which they sat hung down, suspended by its coupling over a bridge.

It was a little while, however, before *Keeping Off The Shelf* made its way across the Atlantic, and meanwhile the Dickens Fellowship was no doubt delighted to hear from Sir George Douglas, guest of honour at their 1929 Annual Conference banquet, that Dickens's 'temperament in relation to the other sex was philoprogenitive rather than amorous'. Sir George continued (as reported in *The Dickensian*):

> His sentiment for Maria Beadnell, as for Ellen Ternan, has been subjected to minute analysis without disclosing a tittle of unworthy motive. And really, I think that the time has come to warn off the revelation-hunter from the Dickens preserve!

Sir George does not mention where exactly he had seen 'minute analysis' of Dickens's feelings for Maria and for Ellen, but no one at that Edinburgh banquet was going to cross-question him about that.

When Blanche Whiffen's book appeared in Britain, the attention of Dickensians naturally focused on her reported gossip concerning Dickens and his 'god-daughter'. The matter was referred to Sir Henry and his unequivocal response appeared in the 1929–30 winter number of *The Dickensian*, in a piece by Ley headed 'Nailing a Lie'. After stressing how 'vague and unreliable' such second-hand reminiscences of far-off days must be, Ley quoted a statement by Sir Henry saying that he had seen reports about Ellen Ternan being his father's god-daughter but that he knew of nothing that justified such a suggestion. As to the statement that she was with him at Staplehurst, that was 'pure invention': 'So far as my own recollection goes there was no one with him at the time, and the statement with regard to her being there I am certain is rubbish.'

Ley ended by offering a reconstruction of how the story is likely to have originated among what he calls the 'small minority of people who whispered spitefully about [Dickens]' during the last ten years of his life:

> There occurred a terrible railway accident in which he escaped death by a miracle. It became known there was a young woman in his compartment at the time. 'Shsh!' said these people mysteriously. 'There you are! Ellen Ternan!' What more natural than that a lad in the choir at Rochester Cathedral should hear this? Years later he marries and, of course, recalls to his wife his memories of Dickens. No doubt he tells her what he remembers being whispered at the time. Pretty well half a century later, when he himself has been dead several years, his widow recalls all this.

It is the kind of thing, writes Ley with his eye on Bechhofer Roberts, that, if it were to go uncontradicted, might play into the hands of another writer 'with a desire for *réclame* plus a spite towards Dickens'.

By the time that Sir Henry issued his robust denial that Ellen Ternan had been his father's fellow-passenger on that ill-fated tidal train to London on 9 June 1865, he was Dickens's only surviving child. Georgina Hogarth had died in 1917, having outlived Ellen by two years, and Kate Perugini died in 1929, so that at the age of eighty-one he was now the last of the Guardians of the Beloved Memory and his sudden death four years later would lead to a lively resurgence of the Great Dickens Scandal at the very heart of Britain's mass media.

Chapter postscript

It is pleasing to record that *The Portsmouth News* for 24 October 2011 carried, under a headline reading 'Banned novel is back on the Portsmouth library shelves', the news that Bechhofer Roberts's *This Side Idolatry,* which had been banished from the library's shelves in 1928, had now been 'welcomed back'. The Library's Literature Development Officer was reported as saying, 'We've decided it's time to let bygones be bygones'.

CHAPTER FOUR

1934–1938
Boiling over

The year 1934 marked a turning-point in the history of the Dickens scandal. On 16 December 1933 Sir Henry Dickens was knocked down by a motorcyclist on the Chelsea Embankment and died of his injuries five days later. He was Dickens's last surviving child and the popular press suddenly became even more Dickens-minded. There was already a heightened awareness of Dickens in the minds of newspaper editors and proprietors because of the circulation war then being waged between some of the leading dailies in which Dickens's works were providing the ammunition – a remarkable indication of the cultural status they still enjoyed in the eyes of the general British public. This war had been sparked off by the *Daily Herald*'s offer to give registered readers a sixteen-volume set of Dickens worth four guineas (eighty-four shillings) for a mere eleven shillings. In his *The Thirties* Malcolm Muggeridge records that after this 'the *Daily Mail, Daily Express* and *News Chronicle* offered their readers sets of Dickens's works for ten shillings, and disposed of 120,000, 124,000 and 65,000 sets respectively at an average loss of £1,200 per 10,000 sets'. The Summer 1934 issue of *The*

Dickensian reported, 'It is estimated that six million copies of Dickens's novels were disposed of in about three months'. Now, however, Sir Henry's death provided an opportunity for a newspaper to exploit Dickens as a circulation-booster in a quite different and less costly way – a way, moreover, that rivals would be unable to imitate.

It was known that Dickens had written a life of Christ for his children which had not been intended for publication. It was also known that the manuscript, titled *The Children's New Testament*, was still owned by the Dickens family. Dickens's children had respected their father's embargo on publication, but Sir Henry had said that he saw no reason why the next generation should feel itself similarly bound and this was soon known in Fleet Street. Several newspapers were eager to acquire the first serial rights, sight unseen, but Cecil Hunt, the enterprising fiction editor of Lord Rothermere's *Daily Mail*, stole a march on his colleagues by the swiftness with which he contacted Sir Henry's two eldest sons. In his *Ink In My Veins* Hunt describes how he obtained from them an understanding that the *Mail* would receive some kind of preferential treatment when it came to disposing of the serial rights. This must have quickly become common knowledge in Fleet Street, so it was perhaps not surprising that *The Daily Express*, organ of Rothermere's rival press baron Lord Beaverbrook, should on 23 January run a full-page 'spoiler' article headed 'The Private Life of Charles Dickens. A Genius With His Human Side', written by no less an authority than Ralph Straus, and implicitly calling into question Dickens's credentials as a good practising Christian.

With Sir Henry now safely dead, Straus evidently no longer felt the need for the kind of discretion he had exercised five years earlier in his *Portrait in Pencil*. He was, he wrote, constantly being asked, 'What is all this mystery about Dickens's private life? . . . now that all his children are dead, surely . . . the truth may be told?' His answer to this was that the truth was 'not really very dreadful', nor was it all that shocking if people would but recognise that 'besides being a towering genius Dickens was also a man'. He went on, in an article full of man-of-the-world nudges and winks, to invoke the name of the 'pretty actress' Ellen Lawless Ternan and to claim, on the evidence of some 'family letters' he had seen (presumably the same ones as he had referred to in his *Portrait*), that Dickens had been less than wholly truthful in his 'Personal' statement about the spotless virtue of the young lady whose name had been linked with his in 1858. But, Straus with some casuistry insists, Dickens was not being hypocritical. He was merely taking the necessary steps to defend his public persona, that 'Grand Production of Charles Dickens' to which his whole life was devoted and on which his livelihood depended. Though not 'vicious', wrote Straus, Dickens was 'certainly no saint' and 'in his later years' enjoyed frequenting 'a careless Bohemian world' where he met 'attractive young actresses whom he would playfully call "little periwinkles"'.

Straus's article is accompanied by a reproduction of Augustus Egg's painting of Georgina Hogarth as an attractive, submissive-looking young woman bent over her sewing, with a caption stating that her continuing position in Dickens's household was 'seized upon by the scandalmongers'. Also shown was an image of the handsome young Dickens flanked by two pictures of almost identical fat-faced matrons, one labelled 'Maria Beadnell, Dickens' first love' (she is not mentioned in the article, in fact) and the other 'Mrs Dickens'. The latter, Straus writes, may have been loved by Dickens when she was young (when, however, he had also loved her younger sister Mary), but she 'was no wife for a world-famous novelist', being as she was, 'a placid lady, perhaps rather too placid', who was glad 'to give [her children] over into Georgina's care'. Straus concludes by asserting that in the late 1850s Dickens, by then yearning to be freed from his marriage, began to find, under the guidance of raffish Wilkie Collins, what Straus delicately refers to as 'new fields of relaxation', thereby leading to 'accusations' on the part of Dickens's in-laws. Although the Hogarths were 'induced to recant' these accusations, Straus confesses himself unable to believe that they can have been 'wholly groundless' and he ends by giving the reader a final hefty nudge:

And henceforth Dickens was without a wife.

Is it very difficult to understand the truth?

Then, on the day following the publication of Straus's article, the *Express* featured in its correspondence columns a lively letter from a certain A. E. Stamford of Coventry deploring the 'pittance' Dickens allowed his wife after their separation while he, 'the great lofty-minded Dickens . . . was philandering with the "periwinkles", the cheap actresses who fawned upon him'. Mr Stamford goes on to make the bizarre assertion that Dickens 'left "Lollipop" (one of these creatures) more in his will than the mother of his ten children . . .'. The next day appeared a letter from a Mr A. Cripps of Worthing who asked, 'Why should Mr R. Straus . . . hesitate to call the famous author a hypocrite?' After all, 'the fact that Dickens wrote so sympathetically of a hypocrite (namely Pecksniff) suggests strongly that there was a strain of hypocrisy in his own character'.

While the *Express* was doing its best to queer the pitch for the *Mail*'s presentation of Dickens's retelling of the life of Christ, another popular paper, this time one of the Sundays, was eager to get in on the Dickens act. In 1933 Walter Dexter, armed with a resolution passed by the Dickens Fellowship's Executive Committee, had finally persuaded Sir Henry to agree to the English publication in full of his father's letters to Maria Beadnell. Their publication was needed, declared the Fellowship, to 'protect the name of Dickens' because it would end lurid speculation about just what those asterisks in *The Strand Magazine* might have been concealing. Sir Henry having proposed that all fees received for publication should go to the Fellowship, Dexter engaged the services of a literary agent in order to get the best terms. Once it became known, however, that nothing sensational had lurked behind the asterisks, media interest in the Beadnell letters waned and refocused on those letters of Dickens to his wife that had been deposited in the British Museum by Kate Perugini. With Sir Henry's death the ban on their publication no longer applied and at the start of 1934 there was intense press speculation about what secrets of Dickens's emotional history they might reveal and about whether the Dickens family would ever allow their publication. This, and the surge of excitement over Dickens's *Children's New Testament*, meant that any unpublished, or hitherto only privately published, material relating to the great man's love-life, no matter how innocent, was of keen interest to the media and the stock of the Beadnell letters rose again.

Dexter's phone was jammed with reporters 'ringing all day long on matters Dickensian'. Among these he was delighted to get a call from an agent saying that *The Sunday Graphic* was offering no less than £400 for the first serial rights. He accepted and Dickens's letters to Maria Beadnell were duly serialised in the *Graphic* from 21 January to 25 February 1934, illustrated by some splendid period sketches of the dramatis personae by John Pisani in a style anticipating the memorable covers he was to design a few years later for Peter Cheyney's hardboiled detective novels. His illustration for the final instalment seems to have been inspired by some words in the last letter that Dickens wrote to Maria. Responding on 17 November 1862 to the news of her father's death, Dickens writes consolingly that 'he died among his children'. Pisani depicts Dickens himself lovingly surrounded by four of his children (presumably meant for Charley, Mamie, Katey and Henry, the four who were still in England in his last years) but the head of a doleful-looking Catherine floating in a cloud to the right of the happy group is there to remind the *Sunday Graphic*'s readers of the Dickens marital breakdown of 1858 and all the scandalmongering to which it gave rise.

Meanwhile, the *Mail* had succeeded in closing the deal with the Dickens family, paying £40,000 for the first serial rights of the 14,000-word manuscript of *The Children's New Testament*, also for the right to publish it in book form under the title *The Life of Our Lord*, which makes it clear that the work relates only to the Gospels. The *Mail*'s preliminary publicity was, recalled Cecil Hunt, on an unprecedented scale in that it included 'every form of displayed advertisement, screen announcements, leaflets and letters by the million, addressed to every minister of religion, superintendents of Sunday schools, youth clubs, etc.'. According to Muggeridge's *The Thirties*, 'posters appeared in the tube stations and other prominent places of Dickens's head looking out from under a crown of thorns'. The eagerly-anticipated first instalment appeared on 5 March. It was captioned in Gothic type and illustrated by a reproduction of Holman Hunt's 'The Light of the World'. A framed notice announced that the paper was 'deeply sensible' of the honour it enjoyed in presenting 'the most beautiful Life Story the world will ever know'. It represented 'the only unpublished work of the great novelist' and 'never was his precious pen more nobly employed'. That morning the paper shifted about 250,000 extra copies.

The *Express*, having already done its best to besmirch Dickens's reputation in January, was not long in launching what it hoped would be its spoiling counter-sensation. In its 3 April issue, under the rather lumbering and unpromising headline '98 Years Ago To-day – Charles Dickens Began His Honeymoon', Wright at last spilled those beans he had been hoarding for nearly forty years. How did he get his *entrée* to the *Express*? With both Bechhofer Roberts and Ralph Straus being connected with the paper, the answer might be that one of them had told Beaverbrook about him. Beaverbrook at once decided, according to Muggeridge's *The Infernal Grove*, 'to punish Rothermere's *Daily Mail* for having acquired at great expense exclusive rights in Dickens's *Life of Christ* by publishing Thomas Wright's disclosures about Dickens's affair with Ellen Ternan'. This would explain the seemingly irrelevant photograph of Dickens's modest Portsmouth birthplace that accompanies Wright's article, with a caption rather pointedly referring to the *Mail*'s expensive purchase: 'Sixty-four years after his death an unpublished Dickens manuscript was recently sold for about £40,000. Genius can be born in very little houses.' Wright's actual article begins: 'All men, and some women, are liable to err. . . . Charles Dickens made two ghastly mistakes. On one of them I can throw a light.' Given the title of his piece, the implication would seem to be that one of Dickens's mistakes was his marriage, but it transpires that the two mistakes were his relationship with Ellen and his decision to turn professional public reader of his own works.

Wright notes that he began working on a Dickens biography in 1893 and received much help from F. G. Kitton and W. R. Hughes, as well as from John Hollingshead and Percy Fitzgerald, two more of 'Dickens's young men'. He had received strong encouragement and valuable – not to say sensational – information from a certain Canon William Benham. Benham, the trusted confidant of two successive Archbishops of Canterbury, had a strong literary bent. He had produced an edition of the letters of William Cowper and greatly admired Wright's biography of this poet. Benham was a great Dickens enthusiast, a Vice-President of the Dickens Fellowship, and a notable giver of public readings from Dickens's work for charitable causes. When he died in 1910 he was eulogised in *The*

Dickensian. It was on the authority of this eminent Dickensian that Wright now presented as historical fact the scene from Bechhofer Roberts's novel in which Dickens first encounters Ellen backstage at the theatre in distress over her too-revealing stage costume. If Benham is indeed Wright's source for this unlikely scene, we must wonder where Bechhofer Roberts had got the story from, assuming he did not simply invent it (which is almost certainly what he did). Wright also includes a version of the story about the jewellery intended by Dickens for Ellen but delivered to Catherine by mistake, and attributes this also to Benham. He states, still citing the deceased Canon as his authority, that Dickens's relationship with Ellen was technically innocent at the time of his separation from Catherine. They might, Wright opines, have stayed simply friends, which would have 'brightened' Dickens's life, nor would his later novels have then been 'shrouded in gloom'. Dickens made the mistake, however, of seducing Ellen and both their lives were 'spoiled' in consequence. Apparently, their sexual liaison was of short duration because of Ellen's distress about it (again, Wright implies that Benham is his authority for this 'fact'):

> Although the close intimacy could not have lasted long [Ellen] was tortured by remorse, and later she took her trouble to Canon Benham, who had become her spiritual adviser. She told him the whole story and declared that she loathed the very thought of the intimacy.
>
> Now if Dickens's conduct spoilt the life of Miss Ternan it certainly went very far to spoiling his own. He could not be happy (how could he?), knowing that Miss Ternan was assailing herself with reproaches and drawing daily further and further from him. They were both of them miserable, and Dickens's unhappiness . . . is reflected in his later books, which can be understood only in the light of this knowledge.

For *Express* readers, invited to relish this moral melodrama, Wright's calling Benham Ellen's 'spiritual adviser' (a phrase he later dropped) must have helped to build up an idea of her as a penitent Magdalen figure.

As a final flourish, Wright asserts that 'at one time much of the story was in danger of being blurted out to the public'. Dickens's eldest son, Charley, 'said more than once, "If my father says anything against my mother, I'll speak out, cost what it will"'. No evidence for such an attitude on Charley's part has ever emerged. He had, however, been evidently concerned to bolster his mother's status in his parents' marriage when he recorded in an 1892 'Introduction' to *David Copperfield* that, contrary to his recorded statement, Dickens had shown the 'Autobiographical Fragment' to Catherine and had allowed her to persuade him not to publish it because he had written so harshly about his parents, and especially about his mother.

By comparison with the effect of the publication of *This Side Idolatry* six years earlier, Wright's article seems to have been rather a damp squib. A couple of readers, one of them a nephew of Benham in fact, wrote in to the *Express* (5 April) to deplore the late Canon's apparent gross and unprofessional betrayal of Ellen's confidence, but otherwise there seems to have been very little public response. *The Dickensian* simply ignored Wright's article and the *Mail* continued imperturbably with its high-profile serialisation of *The Life of Our Lord*. We should not be surprised, perhaps, that the book-buying public of the day was more overtly responsive to a literary sensation such as *This Side Idolatry*'s assault on the moral character of the great and good Charles Dickens than were readers of the popular press to such tittle-tattle as Wright's. That this was indeed the case would seem to be borne out by the stir caused that autumn by Wishart and Co.'s publication of a new and highly critical biography called *The Sentimental Journey: A Life of Charles Dickens* by Hugh Kingsmill.

Kingsmill, who already had some form as an iconoclastic biographer, seems to have been provoked into writing his Dickens biography by G. K. Chesterton's roistering celebrations of Dickens and had been stimulated also by Wright's *Express* article, which he hailed in a prefatory note to *The Sentimental Journey* as 'the most important contribution to the biography of Dickens in this century'. In Kingsmill's view, Dickens, following his rejection by Maria Beadnell, had become 'an incurable emotional hypochondriac' with a 'core of implacable self-love at the centre of his nature'. Kingsmill adopts Wright's anecdotes and his report of Dickens's involvement with 'little periwinkles' (this detail Wright seems to have taken from Ralph Straus's article in the *Express* of 23 January). In the last thirty pages of his biography, Kingsmill develops from Wright's concluding assertion in his *Express* article that Dickens's later books can only be understood in the light of his involvement with Ellen, a contention that soon became a commonplace in biographical-critical Dickens studies. This was that Ellen herself and Dickens's relations with her are reflected in certain leading female characters in his last novels. These characters are cold Estella in *Great Expectations* whose 'insolence and capriciousness no doubt reflect Miss Ternan's contempt for her middle-aged lover and resentment against him'; the mercenary Bella of the earlier part of *Our Mutual Friend*; and emotionally volatile Helena Landless in *Edwin Drood*. Dickens likens Helena's whole physical expression to a kind of 'pause' that could equally well precede 'a crouch or a bound', which two words, says Kingsmill,

> probably sum up Ellen Ternan in her relation to Dickens. When she was frightened of offending him past repair she crouched; when she was exasperated beyond control she bounded; and her fascination perhaps resided in Dickens's perpetual uncertainty which she was about to do.

Kingsmill follows Wright in seeing Dickens's relationship with Ellen as chaste at the time of his separation from Catherine and for a short while afterwards. He goes beyond Wright, however, in contending that she was at first a successor to Mary Hogarth in providing him with an embodiment of 'perfect innocence' (this was before she took to all the crouching and bounding business, presumably), so that while 'the periwinkles answered one of his needs', Ellen, 'by whose shrinking distress he had been enraptured' (that scene from *This Side Idolatry* again!), supplied the other. His subsequent change from worshipping her to desiring her was 'as painful to him as it was irresistible':

In the absence of definite knowledge *one may assume* that he overwhelmed her scruples and his own shortly after the separation from Mrs Dickens. *No doubt* he urged his loneliness, and embraced her in a typhoon of self-pity. [my italics]

It is Kingsmill who first introduces into the Scandal narrative the idea that Ellen was mercenary in her attitude towards her distinguished lover: 'Bella declaiming against her poverty [in *Our Mutual Friend*] and Miss Ternan accepting jewellery from Dickens, are the same person.' From Wright's report of what Benham told him, Kingsmill infers that Ellen had 'wished to get as much benefit from the friendship with [Dickens] as was compatible with not giving herself, and felt deeply resentful when the situation passed beyond her control'. His final belief is that 'though Ellen Ternan appealed at first to [Dickens's] idealism she soon became the object of the sensuality with which he tried to drug the unhappiness of his later years'.

Kingsmill's Dickens biography was widely noticed and won praise for its literary panache. He was much criticised, however, for the crudeness with which he had reconstructed Dickens's emotional history from the evidence of the novelist's fictional creations. The extreme one-sidedness of his approach also came in for criticism, predictably from Chesterton but also later from George Orwell writing in *The New York Times* on 16 May 1949, the day after Kingsmill's death. *The Sentimental Journey* was 'a brilliant book', he wrote, but it was 'the case for the prosecution'. As to Kingsmill's beliefs about Ellen's character being reflected in certain of Dickens's later female characters, the eminent Victorian scholar G. M. Young commented in *The Observer* (25 November 1934) that if she really had been the model for Estella, Bella and Helena, then indeed 'she must have been a mettlesome wench'. Other reviewers such as Bernard Darwin, himself the author of an innocuous little 1933 biography of Dickens, writing in the *Times Literary Supplement* on 22 November, and Ley who deplored the book as 'utterly valueless' in the spring 1935 issue of *The Dickensian*, contrived – amazingly – to avoid all mention of Ellen. Inevitably, some reviewers, like the one in *The Northern Echo* (21 November 1934), wrongly saw Kingsmill as simply 'debunking' Dickens in Lytton Strachey mode, and a number of others unfavourably contrasted his 'psychological' approach to Dickens with the more traditional literary-critical one of André Maurois, an English translation of whose admiring 1928 study of Dickens as man and writer appeared contemporaneously with *The Sentimental Journey*. Maurois mentions only in passing the 'legend' that Dickens's falling in love with Ellen brought about the end of his marriage and comments, 'But it really seems that if, as is possible, Dickens loved this girl, his love remained platonic and Dickensian – the love for the sylph'. We might note that, to avoid bringing blushes to English cheeks, the last five words replace in the English translation of Maurois the following original French text: 'si même il fut sensuel, était-ce bien grave? ('even if it [Dickens's love for Ellen] was physical, was that such a serious matter?'). The Great Dickens Scandal could not take root in Gallic soil. Meanwhile Kingsmill was shocked by the treatment he received from English reviewers: 'I was,' he wrote later, 'I learned with pained surprise from my reviews, a peerer through keyholes, a Freudian dabbling in garbage, and a grave-desecrating ghoul.'

As noted above, 1934 had opened with much feverish press expectation about what sensational secrets of Dickens's emotional life might be revealed when the box of letters to his wife was opened as it now could be, according to Kate Perugini's stipulations, with the death of Sir Henry, Dickens's last surviving child. Speculation was also rife as to whether the Dickens family would sanction the letters' publication. Photographs appeared in the papers of the actual box being contemplated by the British Museum official whose task it was going to be to open it. But as news gradually leaked out that the letters did not, in fact, contain any sensational revelations, interest in them died down and the *Mail's* ongoing serialisation of *The Life Of Our Lord* became the main Dickens story of the day. Meanwhile, the Dickens family agreed to publication of Dickens's letters to Catherine and in the late spring of 1935 they duly appeared in a volume edited by Dexter and entitled *Mr and Mrs Charles Dickens: His Letters to Her*. Dexter contributed a brief introductory note and added a number of appendices presenting documents relevant to the separation such as the 'Violated Letter'. Ellen was, of course, nowhere in sight and D. L. Murray noted approvingly in *The Times Literary Supplement* of 13 June that the letters 'do not feed any scandal'.

Kingsmill's review of *Mr and Mrs Charles Dickens* in the weekly journal *Time and Tide* (6 July 1935) sparked off a controversy between him and Bechhofer Roberts in the journal's correspondence columns about whether or not Dickens had ever loved his wife, Kingsmill having said that these letters clearly showed he had not. Bechhofer Roberts wrote (13 July):

I have never believed a word of Mr Thomas Wright's story that Canon Benham revealed to him that Ellen Ternan had confessed to a sexual relationship with Dickens; canons don't betray such secrets. I never believed the gossip that Dickens and his sister-in-law misbehaved. Nor do I see any reason to accept Mr Kingsmill's wild guess.

Kingsmill hit back by suggesting that Bechhofer Roberts should issue a new edition of his novel with the title *This Side Adultery*. At this point Bernard Shaw intervened, to the delight no doubt of *Time and Tide*'s editor. Wright was silent, either because he was unaware of the controversy, which seems unlikely, or else because he was keeping his powder dry.

Shaw wrote that he had known Kate Perugini and revealed that it was he who had persuaded her to deposit the letters in the British Museum rather than burning them as she had intended to. She had wanted to do this because she thought that they showed the exact opposite of what her mother had hoped they would show, namely that Dickens had once loved her. Kate, no doubt thinking primarily of Dickens's courtship letters which contain several reproofs of Catherine for behaving in ways displeasing or disappointing to him, believed they showed no such thing. On the contrary, Shaw recalled, she believed they showed that Dickens 'had never loved his wife and found out his mistake even before their marriage'. Shaw had told her that, thanks to Ibsen, posterity might well sympathise more with 'the woman who was sacrificed to the genius's uxoriousness to the appalling extent of having had to bear eleven children in sixteen years than with a grievance which, after all, amounted only to the fact that she was not a female Charles Dickens'. Having now read the letters himself, he thought they proved with ridiculous obviousness that Dickens was quite as much in love when he married as nine hundred and ninety-nine out of every thousand British bridegrooms, and that this normal state of things outlasted even the eleven pregnancies.

As to the separation, Shaw evidently accepted Dickens's statement in the 'Violated Letter' that it was Catherine who had for some time been begging him to let her go and that he had come only slowly and reluctantly to the conclusion that it would be better for them to part. It was probably Dickens's ungallant reference in this document to 'a mental disorder under which she [Catherine] sometimes labours' that prompted Shaw's curious speculation that she might have been 'driven crazy by the too rapid exploitation of her fertility'. He makes no reference whatever to Ellen.

Wright's *Life of Charles Dickens*, so long in the gestation, finally made its appearance on 24 September 1935. It was published by Herbert Jenkins, 'a firm noted for their works of fiction', Dexter mischievously noted in the autumn number of *The Dickensian*. Having recalled that Wright's *Express* article, hitherto ignored by *The Dickensian*, had linked Dickens's name with 'that of a young lady called Ellen Ternan', Dexter loftily wondered 'what else Mr Wright has new to tell us to warrant the publication of a new life of Dickens'. Meanwhile, Wright's allegations rested solely on his report of what Canon Benham had told *him*, and Dexter did not believe that 'the average layman would have so poor a regard for a minister of the church as to believe that a priest would be so untrue to his trust', even though another clergyman had recently shown he had no problem over this. Dexter was referring to a certain Rev. A. H. T. Clarke of Devizes, who had written to *The Observer* on 23 June 1935 in response to the paper's review of *Mr and Mrs Charles Dickens*. The Rev. Clarke mentions Wright's forthcoming biography and not only accepts the truth of Wright's report of what Benham told him but even goes a bit beyond it with a reference to Ellen's having 'enticed' Dickens at the time of the separation.

Herbert Jenkins's advertising brochure for Wright's biography described it as 'A New and Exhaustive Life of Charles Dickens' with 'New and intensely interesting particulars'. It would tell 'the whole story of Dickens's life for the first time, including that of his fourteen years intimacy with Miss Ellen Lawless Ternan'. Wright was described as 'absolutely impartial' and as giving 'chapter and verse for all his statements'. Readers of his *Life of Dickens* soon discovered, however, that he was hardly the sort of biographer to confine himself to an impartial statement of the facts. In several places he allows himself considerable imaginative latitude as when, for example, he asserts that by 1846 relations between Dickens and his wife were becoming ever more strained, with Catherine resenting 'as any wife would, the constant placing before her of the virtues of the dead Mary Hogarth', as well as the increasing usurpation of her domestic role by Georgina. By the time Ellen enters the story Wright feels able to assert that Dickens and Catherine had 'long . . . been seriously estranged' and proceeds to give the 'periwinkles' their last but one outing in Dickensian biography: 'Dickens, in those days [c.1856–57] an habitual frequenter of the green rooms in the theatres, was fascinated by the little actresses or "periwinkles" as he called them'. Wright, who, as we have seen, was to confess in his autobiography his especial interest in 'the love experience, regular or irregular, of men of genius', notes, inaccurately, that 'the periwinkle twines round plants just as the human sort takes captive the hearts of mankind'.

In his *Dickens* he repeats as factual history yet again Bechhofer Roberts's fictional anecdote of Dickens's first encounter with Ellen, though this time he does *not* cite Benham as his authority nor, indeed, anyone else. He then proceeds to invent a narrative of

the development of their relationship based on no evidence whatever and indulges in some colourful commentary:

> An intimate friendship between the famous author and the
> young actress followed, a friendship that daily threatened to
> become more than friendship. She was often in his house and
> he liked to have her in his study when he was writing. How
> perilous is the rock named Beauty! What havoc may result
> from a smile, a whiff of scent, a touch – even a tear! Especially
> when mingled with the sob of violins!

Wright also asserts, again with no supporting evidence whatever, that the participation of the Ternans in Dickens's Amateur
Company's fund-raising production of Wilkie Collins's *The
Frozen Deep* was 'gall and bitterness' to Catherine, who 'expressed
herself openly, with the result that the trouble in the house rose
once more to a height'. Certain details in his subsequent account
of the separation show, however, that he must have had access,
perhaps through Ralph Straus, to the long letter from Catherine's
aunt Helen Thomson to a Mrs Stark, a family friend (see above,
p. 31), though he never actually cites it. This letter, which
describes in some detail the breakdown of the marriage from
Catherine's point of view, was for a long time dismissed as a
forgery by Dexter and other Dickensians but was later to be
proved genuine. In a later section of his Dickens biography,
headed 'The Apotheosis of Miss E. L. Ternan', Wright repeats
the Benham-authenticated material from his *Express* article
about Ellen giving herself 'reluctantly' to Dickens after the separation, but now adds a further notable detail, also apparently on
Benham's authority: 'He [Dickens] took for her a house No.2
Houghton Place, Ampthill Square' (near Mornington Crescent).
It seems very odd indeed that Benham should have gone into
this amount of documentary detail when he was allegedly telling

Wright about Ellen's scandalous past, and yet Wright must have got the address from *somewhere* in order to go and check it in the London Directory as he evidently did. It may well be that he got it from Dickens's will and then, either intentionally or as a result of muddle, attributed the information to Benham. It enabled him now to add the detail that Mrs Ternan was listed as the householder from 1861 to 1865 and he did not fail to add some moralising commentary:

> He [Dickens] imagined that he had entered into a new life and that it would be roses, roses all the way. He forgot that roses have thorns. He thought he was in front of the supremest felicity ever enjoyed by mortal man. He wasn't.

At this point Wright incorporates into his narrative, again with no acknowledgement of his source, some purported reminiscences by the recently-deceased composer Francesco Berger, who as a young man had been involved in Dickens's amateur theatrical productions. These reminiscences had been published by Andrew de Ternant two years earlier in *Notes and Queries* and were apparently unknown to Dickensians. According to de Ternant, Berger remembered Sunday evening visits to the Ternan household in the early 1860s when he would play cards with Ellen, Dickens and Mrs Ternan, and play the piano while Ellen and Dickens sang duets. Wright does not seem to see, any more than did later Dickens biographers, including myself, how oddly this cosy picture of cheerful domesticity sorts with the picture of Ellen that he has been painting as what her contemporaries would have called a fallen woman, unhappily 'assailing herself with reproaches' about her relationship with Dickens and 'drawing daily further and further from him'. It was to be a long time before an entirely new light would be cast on this anecdote (see below, p. 184).

For the rest of his *Life of Charles Dickens* Wright seems to have relied for his account of Dickens's relationship with Ellen on his idea that Estella in *Great Expectations*, Bella in *Our Mutual Friend*, and Helena Landless in *Edwin Drood* were all based upon her and reflect aspects of her relationship to Dickens. He insists, with grim relish, on Ellen's coldness and indifference towards a Dickens who was unable to hide from himself the fact 'that her attachment to him was artificial – that she merely endured him'. Ellen's attitude to her distinguished lover, Wright claims, 'is plainly revealed in the descriptions of the various wooings to be found in his last novels'. He seems to have been unaware of Mrs Whiffen's revelation that Ellen had been with Dickens at Staplehurst. He relates an odd anecdote, based on an interview with the late W. R. Hughes, author of *A Week's Tramp in Dickens-land* (1891). Hughes apparently told Wright that he had once been offered for purchase a bundle of Dickens's letters to Ellen. Hughes had said to the would-be vendor that he could not have obtained the letters honestly and advised him to go home and burn them. Wright doubts that Hughes's advice was followed, so that 'some day they [the letters] may come to light'. The world is still waiting.

Wright's rather bumbling book perhaps suffered from following so hard upon the heels of Kingsmill's far more stylishly written biography and seems on the whole to have received fairly perfunctory attention from the national press. The *Times Literary Supplement* notice on 30 November was brief, commending Wright for his zeal in 'collecting and collating masses of material' but doubting if there was really room for another Dickens biography. As to Ellen, the reviewer notes that Benham was Wright's sole authority for her having been Dickens's mistress, and comments, 'opinions may differ on the solidity of such evidence'. The *Spectator* reviewer observes (6 December) that 'not everyone will be inclined to accept [Benham's reported comments] blindly' and *The Saturday Review* (28 December), while it makes favourable mention of Wright's book as a whole, says of the details he supplies concerning Dickens and Ellen that 'since he got them second-hand from Canon Benham, they amount to nothing more than "hearsay"'. The radical journalist Douglas Goldring, writing in the *Liverpool Post* on 6 November, accepts that Wright was reporting Benham accurately but deplores the latter's apparent betrayal of his trust. In his response to this on 13 November Wright produced what he evidently regarded as his trump card. This was a letter Benham had written to him in 1897 saying how pleased he was that Wright was working on a life of Dickens and mentioning that he had a 'curious relic' of the great man, namely the pen he had used to write part of the last number of *Edwin Drood*. Benham's letter ends with these words: 'It [the pen] was given to me by the lady concerning whom he quarrelled with his wife. This between ourselves.' Wright argues that as so much time has passed and Ellen is now dead, as well as all of Dickens's children, he feels himself at liberty to reveal what he claims Benham subsequently told him about the relationship. He blithely adds, 'The words "this between ourselves" in the above quoted letter clear Canon Benham', which is something they can hardly be said to do. As to Ellen's children, who were both still very much alive in 1934, either Wright was unaware of them or he simply did not care what effect his revelations might have upon them.

Ley was not long in responding to Wright's letter, pointing out in *The Liverpool Post* for 26 November that Benham's letter did not at all provide the proof positive of Ellen's having been Dickens's mistress that Wright seemed to think it did. For the next month or two, as can be seen from the Dickens Fellowship scrapbooks held at the Charles Dickens Museum, Ley pursued Wright through a number of journals including *The Scotsman, John O'London's Weekly* and *The Methodist Times*. Whenever a

letter from Wright would appear in one of these papers' correspondence columns (usually thanking the paper's reviewer for a
good review and seeking to defend Benham's reputation),
Ley would respond with a letter denouncing Wright as a
credulous gossip and demanding corroborative evidence for
Benham's alleged statements. Ley also published a seven-page
would-be demolition job in the winter 1935–36 issue of
The Dickensian, headed 'Scandal Articulate At Last', in which
he argued that Wright's assertions regarding Dickens's relationship with Ellen resulted from his having altogether mis-
understood or misinterpreted whatever it was that Benham had
told him.

At this point Bechhofer Roberts intervened in the debate with
a letter to *The Liverpool Post*, accusing both Wright and Ley of
'shadow-boxing'. Like Ley, he called upon Wright to produce
corroborative evidence for Benham's reported words, but he also
demanded that Ley should reveal the reason which he claimed to
know that would explain Dickens's £1,000 legacy to Ellen.
Evidently, he also deemed it a good moment to re-issue *This Side
Idolatry* and it appeared in June under the imprint of Jarrolds.
They were the publishers of a then popular romantic novelist
called Ethel Mannin. She contributed a long prefatory letter to
the re-issue of 'this brave bit of work', recalling 'the flutter in the
literary dovecotes' that it created when it first appeared and 'how
one great Knight of Letters [Sir John Squire, Editor of *John
O'London's Weekly*] wanted you horse-whipped'. *This Side Idolatry*
had stripped 'a sacred public idol' of 'the trappings with which
generations of hero-worship had hung it' and shown the 'unhe-
roic figure underneath'. She reminds Bechhofer Roberts of
how the 'charming romanticism' of Straus's *Portrait in Pencil*
was 'held up as an example to you who had dared to etch in acid
the hard, clear, clean lines of truth' and ends with a ringing
endorsement:

> But here is one who stands by you, as all impatient of the
> sentimentalism of what has become increasingly – since the
> films 'discovered' Dickens – the 'Dickens racket', will stand by
> you with admiration and gratitude.

Mannin's exasperation may remind us that in 1935 three hugely
successful new Dickens films were released, David O. Selznick's
sumptuous M.G.M. productions *A Tale of Two Cities* and *David
Copperfield*, and Twickenham Studios' *Scrooge* with Seymour
Hicks in the title role. The two latter films, in particular, rein-
forced the established public perception of Dickens as the champion of the poor, especially of poor children, and the great
celebrant of the domestic virtues. This would seem to have
remained largely unclouded by literary-world gossip or newspaper scandalmongering.

Meanwhile, Wright, now in his seventy-seventh year, was at
work on his autobiography *Thomas Wright of Olney*. This was
posthumously published in late 1936, Wright having died earlier
that year. In the book he again defended the accuracy of his
account of his interview with Benham and described the method
that he claimed always to use in his biographical researches:

> When interviewing a person I, if possible, write down his
> words in his presence or immediately on leaving his house. I
> have often stood in the street at his door and dotted them
> down for fear of losing anything of importance. . . . My
> memory is a good one, but I never rely on that alone, and I
> took down Canon Benham's words on this occasion. The
> original sheets of paper lie before me at the present moment.
> (pp. 67ff.)

The obvious thing, one might think, would have been for him to
print a transcript of these notes or, better still, to have reproduced

them in facsimile. Instead, he presents a facsimile of the letter from Benham to himself that he had quoted in his *Liverpool Post* exchange with one Douglas Goldring. This letter proves nothing, of course, except that Benham said *something* to Wright about the involvement of another woman in Dickens's separation from Catherine. As to those vaunted 'sheets of paper', scholars have been searching for them ever since, but so far to no avail. No trace of them is to be found in Wright's Dickens archive now preserved at the Charles Dickens Museum in London.

It is also worth noting that Wright says at this point in his *Autobiography*, 'I and my friends had long been aware that Miss Ternan was Dickens's mistress, and that the fact would throw great light on Dickens's latest works'. This strongly suggests that he would have been predisposed to interpret whatever it was that Benham told him about Ellen's relations with Dickens in a sexual way.

He goes on to record, somewhat ungrammatically, what he has learned about Ellen's history subsequent to the publication of his *Life of Charles Dickens*: 'Having received sympathy and comfort from him [Benham], her life, one is pleased to know, became bright again.' It seems Benham had at least had enough discretion in 1897 not to tell Wright that Ellen Ternan had since 1876 been Mrs George Wharton Robinson, as the clear implication of what Wright records here is that her marriage took place some time *after* her confidences to Benham (Wright also states that her husband became principal of Margate High School in 1883 whereas it was actually six years earlier). As to the Robinsons' two children, it seems hard to believe that Wright was completely unaware of their existence. If he did indeed know about them, he certainly showed remarkably little concern about their feelings.

Wright's autobiography contained further Ellen revelations in the form of what its author calls 'a startling story' concerning a hitherto unrecorded address for Dickens. Here he does actually give chapter and verse to support his new information instead of simply asserting the existence of supporting evidence among his papers. The same Rev. A. Clarke who had defended him against the attacks in *The Observer* in the summer of 1935 had, it seems, contacted a certain Mrs Mackie whom he knew to have some 'special knowledge' about Dickens. Mrs Mackie had subsequently written to Wright to tell him that her mother had once employed a Mrs Goldring, who had worked for Dickens when he lived '*sub rosa*' at Linden Grove in the south-eastern London suburb of Nunhead, in a house called Windsor Lodge. Also living there was his 'unofficial wife' who 'was reputed to be a connection of Mr Trollope', an allusion, presumably, to Ellen's sister Fanny, Mrs Thomas Trollope. Wright had interviewed Mrs Mackie and obtained further particulars such as that Mrs Goldring had known her Windsor Lodge employer as 'Mr Tringham' and had known also that he was writing a mystery story, presumably a reference to *The Mystery of Edwin Drood*. Wright had also discovered that there had been a job-master (i.e., hirer of horses and horse-drawn carriages) in Nunhead who well remembered driving Dickens to and from Windsor Lodge. Finally, he had caused a search to be made of the Nunhead rate-books for 1867–70 (subsequently destroyed during World War II), which showed the rates for Windsor Lodge as having been paid successively by 'Frances Turnham', presumably the rate-collector's version of Frances Ternan, Ellen's mother, 'Thomas Turnham' (Frances Ternan's correct title was Mrs Thomas Ternan), 'Thomas Tringham' and 'Charles Tringham'.

According to Ley, reviewing Wright's autobiography in the Winter 1936–37 number of *The Dickensian*, Wright had offered his new discoveries successively to a well-known Sunday newspaper, then a daily paper, and finally 'a literary paper of national standing', but all had declined the offer. And one can see that

Dickens-related stories about what a certain lady had told Wright that her mother's charlady had once told her, and about suggestive names found in old rate-books, would have had rather less appeal to newspaper editors than a story directly told by a distinguished clergyman about Dickens and a penitent mistress. So this new material first appeared in Wright's autobiography, spatchcocked in as a last-minute addition to a somewhat jumbled last chapter. It does not seem to have caught the attention of reviewers, being hardly mentioned in any of the notices of Wright's autobiography that I have seen. These were generally favourable, relishing Wright as a character and praising him for the industrious 'gleanings' he had gathered concerning the lives of the famous as he tracked down 'the relations, friends, acquaintances and even the domestic servants of the dead, and extracted gossip' (*Times Literary Supplement*, 21 November 1936).

In *The Dickensian*, Ley sought to dismiss Wright's latest discoveries as yet more second-hand gossip that was in some respects self-evidently absurd. Meaning to show just how wildly irresponsible Wright had allowed himself to become, Ley quotes (in capital letters) a phrase from letters Wright had written both to him and to Dexter. Wright had apparently written 'There were children' and Ley asks why this claim is not repeated in the autobiography, the implication being that Wright knew he would have been going too far if he had included it. Ironically, it was thus Ley who first introduced what was subsequently to become a leading strand in the scandal, the idea that Dickens and Ellen might have had offspring. Ley ended his piece by countering Wright's reported evidence with some counterbalancing reported evidence of his own. He was by this time in touch with Ellen's daughter Gladys – her son Geoffrey steadfastly refused to have any involvement in the matter for a reason that did not become part of the record until many years later – and she was his authority for the following statement:

... there yet live the two sisters of one who was Ellen's devoted servant and companion for some years before her marriage, her friend afterwards and her children's nurse. And this is what they said to Ellen's daughter, 'Our sister more than once said to us "Tell [Gladys], if she ever asks, that I never mentioned the matter to her because it could only give her pain, but that if she had ever asked me, I should have been able to say solemnly that her dear mother never was the mistress of Charles Dickens"'.

Two years after the appearance of Wright's autobiography the Nonesuch Press, a private press founded by Francis Meynell in 1923 and celebrated for its fine editions, published a remarkably elegant limited edition of Dickens's works in twenty-three volumes at the price per set of 48 guineas (£50.8s.). The last three volumes were devoted to Dickens's letters, edited by Walter Dexter, and represented the first attempt to collect and publish, in unexpurgated form, all known surviving letters of Dickens. The Nonesuch Letters also marked Ellen Ternan's first appearance in the documentary record of Dickens's life since the publication of his will in 1870. No letters to her were to be found in the edition – unsurprisingly, if Wright's anecdote about W. R. Hughes is to be believed, and the would-be vendor of Dickens's letters to her did indeed take his strange advice. However, 'Ternan, Ellen Lawless' does have two entries in the index in addition to the one referring to the will. The first refers to a letter from Dickens to his manservant John dated 25 June 1865 which instructs him to take 'Miss Ellen tomorrow morning, a little basket of fresh fruit, a jar of clotted cream from Tuckers, and a chicken, a pair of pigeons, or some nice little bird' and to repeat this on certain other days, 'making a little variety each day'. Dexter noticeably fails to connect this with the Staplehurst accident, the letter to Mitton describing which (see above, p. 43) had still not been printed in full. The second reference is to a remarkably agitated, and still not satisfactorily explicated, letter incorrectly dated by Dexter to 5 July 1866 (it should be 1867) from Dickens to his intimate and rather excitable amateur-actress friend Frances Elliot, whom he was patiently advising about her own rather chaotic marital affairs. She had evidently stumbled on some information about Ellen's history known only to Dickens and perhaps some one or two other very close friends. Elliot seems to have referred to Ellen and Dickens himself as forming part of a 'magic circle'. She was perhaps offering to visit Ellen to show support. Dickens tells her that 'the "magic circle" consists of but one member', also that 'it would be inexpressibly painful to N to think that you knew her history'. 'She would', he continues, 'not believe that you could see her with my eyes, or know her with my mind. . . . It would distress her for the rest of her life.' He refers to sufferings that Ellen has had to undergo all alone, upheld only by her own 'pride and self-reliance' which is 'mingled' in her gentle nature. Dexter leaves 'N' severely unannotated, so that the reader, turning to this page, is left to work out by a process of elimination that this initial must account for the 'Ternan, Ellen Lawless' reference, though a footnote does identify a 'Mrs T.T.' mentioned with some hostility in the letter as 'Mrs Tom Trollope, *née* Frances Eleanor Ternan'.

Also in the Nonesuch Edition is an eye-catching summary, taken from a sale-catalogue, of a post-Staplehurst letter written to the Head Stationmaster at Charing Cross on 12 June 1865. Dexter may or may not have suspected that the full text would reveal a connection with Ellen, but fortunately for him he was not required to speculate. The sale-catalogue summary he quotes begins as follows: 'Writes about a gold watch, chain, charm, and other trinkets, which were lost by a lady in the same carriage with him [i.e. Dickens], in the railway accident'. It was not until 1952 that a fuller text of the letter appeared in Edgar Johnson's magisterial biography of Dickens, including the tell-tale detail that among the lady's lost trinkets was 'a gold seal engraved "Ellen"'.

Thus discreetly edited, there was little enough in the Nonesuch Letters volumes to feed the Great Dickens Scandal and in his review of them in the Winter 1938–39 issue of *The Dickensian* Ley could exult, 'At every turn the ghouls are thwarted'. But, just as the sumptuous Nonesuch Edition was being distributed to its gratified subscribers, there landed on Dexter's desk the manuscript of a book that threatened to re-ignite the Scandal in a highly sensational manner.

CHAPTER FIVE

1939
His daughter's voice

The manuscript that landed on Dexter's desk was entitled *Dickens and Daughter* and was the work of a former actress called Gladys Storey. Ten years earlier she had written a piece for *The Evening News* of 29 May 1929 reporting the death in her ninetieth year of Dickens's second daughter Kate Perugini. Storey had written of Kate's 'charming personality, her wit and humour, and her great gift for friendship'. She wrote also of Kate's close involvement in the mainstream world of Victorian art in the latter years of the nineteenth century, both in her own right and through her two marriages, first to the Pre-Raphaelite artist Charles Collins, brother of Wilkie, and secondly to the Italian-born portrait-painter Carlo Perugini. Storey herself came from that world, having been born in 1886 the daughter of George Adolphus Storey, a historical painter and member of the so-called 'St John's Wood Clique', a sort of under-sect of the Pre-Raphaelites. During the 1920s Storey and her mother had become close friends of the widowed Mrs Perugini, visiting her regularly on Sunday evenings in her little Chelsea flat.

During this last decade of her long life Kate seems to have become greatly troubled by memories of what seemed to her the unkind way her mother had been treated during the separation crisis and also of her own failure to take Catherine's part. She seems to have often spoken about this to the Storeys just as she had earlier done to Shaw (see above, p. 82). To Shaw she had written in a much less stricken vein and had yielded eventually to his insistence that her mother's hoard of letters from Dickens should be deposited in the British Museum. She had, according to *Dickens and Daughter*, written a life of her father but had burnt it because it 'told only half the truth' and 'a half-truth is worse than a lie'. She would often say, however, 'the truth *must be told* when the time comes – after my death' and, according to Storey, lived in dread of revelations being made during her lifetime in which the facts would come out 'all wrong' because those making them would have only partial knowledge. It was at her most earnest request that Storey had solemnly promised her that after her death she would publish the 'unvarnished truth' as she had heard it from Kate's own lips. Now, with the publication of *Dickens and Daughter*, Storey was, somewhat belatedly, fulfilling that promise. Her publisher, Frederick Muller, evidently felt somewhat anxious about the work and asked Walter Dexter to vet it. Dexter duly did so and subsequently met for three hours with Storey at Muller's office. Afterwards, he wrote two long and detailed letters (now in the archives of the Charles Dickens Museum) about the manuscript itself and about his meeting with Storey, to the great French Dickens scholar-collector and patron of the Dickens Museum, Comte Alain de Suzannet.

Dexter told Suzannet that he had found Storey to be 'very "temperamental"' but was wholly convinced by her claim that she was in the book truthfully reporting things Kate had told her during their many years of fireside chats. When Dexter asked her why she had waited so long to publish, she replied that she had thought it decent to wait until after Sir Henry's death and she had also wished its publication to coincide with the tenth anniversary of Kate's death. During the conversation no reference whatever seems to have been made, strangely enough, by either Dexter or by Storey to *This Side Idolatry* nor to the 'scandalous' Dickens biographies of Thomas Wright and Hugh Kingsmill. Nor is there a word about any of these writers in *Dickens and Daughter* itself, yet it seems hardly possible that Storey can have been unaware of them. Clearly she was concerned above all to tell the story of Kate's relations with Dickens rather than Ellen's.

Wanting to convince Suzannet that Storey was not concerned with scandalous material as such but only with what she had been told and asked to make public by Kate Perugini, Dexter mentioned in his letter a couple of other sensational items that Storey had told him and which she had learned not from Kate but from Sir Henry. The first was that Geoffrey Robinson had come to Sir Henry 'with some letters' and asked him, 'Was my mother your father's mistress?', an anecdote that was not to become public knowledge until 1980 minus the detail about the letters (see below, ch. 8) which, Storey told Dexter, she thought it possible that Geoffrey had blackmailed Sir Henry into buying. The second was that Sir Henry had told her that the family possessed a doctor's certificate to show that Georgina was a virgin, something Dexter said he had heard from Matz 'years before'. Presumably Sir Henry had told B.W. Matz about this document in 1908 when he was speaking to him about the audacious fraud attempted by Charley Peters claiming to be the illegitimate son of Dickens and Georgina Hogarth. It perhaps formed part of the 'supporting evidence' against Peters that Sir Henry told Matz he had sent out to Calcutta.

Storey's book as published begins with a somewhat rambling first chapter which paints a picture of Kate in extreme old age. The next four chapters read very much as though *Dickens and Daughter* were a straight Dickens biography presenting a number of hitherto unknown details and documents about Dickens's father's career in the Navy Pay Office derived from archival research carried out by Storey herself. These chapters take Dickens up to the date of his marriage. Chapter 6 then jumps forward to 1844, when he was living with his family in Genoa, and describes his intense mesmeric treatment of an unnamed lady (later discovered to be Mme De la Rue, English wife of a Swiss banker) who was suffering from distressing hallucinations. Chapter 7 dwells on the domestic happiness of the Dickens family in the 1840s and early 1850s 'before inside and outside influences evolved and brushed away the sweetness of life'. Chapter 8 contains the bombshell. In it Storey, presumably following Kate's oral version of her father's life-history, sees the fondly remembered Maria Beadnell's reappearance as fat loquacious Mrs Henry Winter as the event that led directly to the break-up of the Dickens marriage: 'something had been awakened within him; a something which remained peculiarly, unconsciously expectant of some fulfilment'. This was his state, Storey writes, when as a result of his need to recruit professional actresses for his amateur production of Wilkie Collins's drama *The Frozen Deep*,

Miss Ellen Lawless Ternan, 'the small fair-haired rather pretty actress' (as Mrs Perugini described her), of no special attraction save her youth, came like a breath of spring into the hardworking life of Charles Dickens – and enslaved him. She flattered him – he was ever appreciative of praise – and though 'she was not a good actress she had brains, which she used to educate herself, to bring her mind more on a level with his own. Who could blame her?' said Mrs Perugini in her generous make-excuses way. 'He had the world at his feet. She was a young girl of eighteen, elated and proud to be noticed by him.' Happy at first, perhaps, to love and be loved by him, who subsequently brought to her relief from a hitherto hard and precarious life.

This is certainly a very different picture of Dickens's relationship with Ellen and hers with him from the one painted by Wright and Kingsmill. Ellen herself appears as rather more proactive and more happily complicit in the affair than she does in Wright's description of it – though Storey does go on to say that Ellen came to regret the affair after Dickens's death when 'she married a clergyman and became the mother of his children'.

Storey's comment about Ellen's later regrets concerning her connection with Dickens would seem to corroborate Wright's story of her seeking some kind of spiritual comfort from Canon Benham. But then follows rather more startling confirmation – at least in part – of something that Thomas Wright had *not* published but only written in a letter to Ley, who had printed it, derisively, in *The Dickensian*: 'There were children.' 'More tragic and far-reaching in its effects', declares Storey, 'was the association of Charles Dickens and Ellen Ternan and their resultant son (who died in infancy) than that of Nelson and Lady Hamilton and their daughter.' The invocation of Nelson and Lady Hamilton and their illegitimate daughter Horatia is probably a romantic gloss supplied by Storey herself, but the terse, almost throwaway, reference to Dickens and Ellen's having had a child and to its dying in infancy (contrast Wright's vague phrase, 'there were children') must derive direct from Kate herself and it introduced a thrilling new twist into the tale. Dexter told Suzannet he had asked Storey how this illegitimate birth could have been kept so secret, whereupon she wittily remarked that nobody need know [about a pregnancy] in those days, a crinoline covering a multitude of sins; and she [Ellen] was away in an outlying district in London – Peckham – and there was no fine for the non-registration of babies until 1874. (She has that information in writing from the Registrar of Births etc., Somerset House.)

As we shall see later, the game of 'cherchez l'enfant' was to become, and still remains, a favourite pastime for Dickens scholars, both professional and amateur.

Storey's mention of Peckham confirmed, as Dexter reminded Suzannet, Wright's last Ternan discoveries as presented in his posthumous autobiography. But her statement in *Dickens and Daughter* that it was while the legal arrangements for Dickens's separation from Catherine were being made that 'a settlement was made on Ellen Ternan, who subsequently lived in an establishment of her own at Peckham' was certainly incorrect. Here Kate would seem – not surprisingly, given her age – to have been telescoping certain events in her memory. She forgot – or possibly, unlikely as it seems, she had never known about – Ellen's time in her own house in Mornington Crescent and her subsequent residence with her mother in Slough before her move to Nunhead, which is adjacent to Peckham, in 1867. Kate did vividly recall, however, that at some point before the separation she had found her weeping mother putting on her bonnet as she prepared to go at Dickens's behest and make a courtesy call on Ellen, and how she (Kate) had stamped her foot and said, 'You shall not go!' but all to no avail. Following this there are only a few scattered references to Ellen in the rest of *Dickens and Daughter*. She is mentioned as having been at Gad's Hill, just before one of Kate's own visits, and as having 'taken a hand at cricket' there. Storey must at this point have misread her own notes (which remained unpublished until 1980) as she attributes to Kate her own somewhat feline observation, 'I am afraid she did not play the game!' She quotes Kate as having said she believed that, 'had her father married Maria Beadnell or Ellen Ternan, the ultimate result would have been the same, for he "did not understand women"'. Storey repeats this arresting phrase a few pages later and it has since stood many a Dickens biographer in good stead. The last reference to Ellen in *Dickens and Daughter* occurs when she is mentioned as having visited Gad's Hill (presumably at Georgina and Mamie's invitation) during the afternoon following Dickens's death. The remaining 93 pages of Storey's 236-page book are devoted firstly to the circumstances regarding the publication of *The Life Of Our Lord* and then to the later lives of Catherine Dickens and her children.

Dickens and Daughter was published on 13 July and was reviewed the same day in *The Daily Herald* by Tom Darlow who, back in the 1920s, had worked with Bechhofer Roberts on the aborted biography that had become *This Side Idolatry*. Under the banner headline 'Dickens' daughter speaks at last', Darlow wrote of Storey's book, 'It will certainly cause a tremendous sensation and scandal', since it tells in his daughter's own words 'the carefully and long-concealed truth of Charles Dickens' separation from his wife, and of his well-established association with Miss Ellen Lawless Ternan, who was his mistress for many years and bore him a son who died in infancy'. Once again, Wright and his star witness Canon Benham are mysteriously written out of the record. Storey's revelations are presented as sensationally new and fresh, also as being bound to put an end to the 'great campaign' begun in 1858 'to make [Dickens] out a model husband and father, the pattern embodiment of the Victorian virtues', a 'complete fabrication' which had been 'strenuously maintained' by the members of the Dickens Fellowship and other enthusiasts. 'Most of them', writes Darlow, 'certainly believed what they said. Others, I am afraid, certainly knew the truth.' His conclusion smacks of wishful thinking:

> Now that [Kate] has spoken through Miss Storey's book, we can put the great Dickens cult where it belongs, in the dust bin, and go back to read the superb humour, fun and liveliness of the first of English novelists and the greatest newspaper reporter who ever used a stick of copy.

Little did Darlow suspect that it would not be Dickens's humour and fun alone that would keep his stock high during the next twenty years but also his 'cult', as well as a continuing fascination with his secret life with Ellen, about which, Darlow seems to imply, there was now nothing more to be said.

In fact, Storey's book seems to have caused very little stir. People had, after all, other things to think about in the summer of 1939. Bernard Darwin commented in *The Times Literary Supplement* on 22 July that it really added nothing to what was already known (again, no reference is made to Wright) and opined that it could have been justified only if it had given us a fuller picture of Ellen: 'a girl of eighteen or nineteen who enslaves a great genius of five-and-forty possesses an historical interest which may make permissible such revelations'. But Storey, Darwin complains, gives us very little clue as to Ellen's character: 'she flits for the moment colourless across the stage and might have been left in peace'. Darwin's implication that Kate was in her dotage when confiding in Storey prompted Shaw to make his second public intervention in the ongoing discussion of Dickens's marriage. A letter from him appeared in *The Times Literary Supplement* on 29 July stating that he had had two conversations with Kate about her parents' domestic woes, one forty years before and the other only four months before her death when, he declared, her mind had not been in the least enfeebled. Storey, he said, was certainly carrying out Kate's wishes in publishing the book, even though 'the facts of the case may be in bad taste' – but then, he added with characteristic Shavian impishness, 'facts often are'.

It was left to Ley in the autumn number of *The Dickensian* to put the best face possible on the matter as far as the Dickens Fellowship was concerned. Writing more in sorrow than in anger, he deplores the fact that Kate had left it to others to tell the story of the injustice done to her mother and of her father's alleged liaison with Ellen: 'I should have honoured her [Kate's] memory more if she had carried out her first intention and given the world the story while she was here to witness its truth'. Rather confusingly, he says almost immediately afterwards that Kate should have kept to her 'original intention of holding the whole story back till fifty years after her death' for the sake of Ellen's daughter who was still alive. He does not venture even to mention Ellen's son, Geoffrey Robinson, who, as noted above, chose to remain grimly silent on the subject of his family history – unsurprisingly, in view of his momentous interview with Sir Henry. On one important biographical point, however, Ley does concur with Kate as reported by Storey, though he does so without admitting what he is doing. He, too, believes, as he had argued in the notes to his 1928 edition of Forster's *Life of Dickens*, that it was the reappearance in Dickens's life of Maria Beadnell rather than the appearance of Ellen that spelled the beginning of the end for the Dickens marriage. About Ellen herself Ley says as little as possible and, once again, all of Wright's discoveries and speculations go completely unmentioned.

They could hardly be ignored, however, any more than Storey's book could be, by that redoubtable woman of letters Dame Una Pope-Hennessy, whose biography *Charles Dickens: 1812–1870* appeared in 1945. She cites both Wright and Storey, registering a certain distaste for the former, however, by noting that he 'made a speciality of discoveries in the private lives of the eminent' and describing him as having 'nosed out the Peckham establishment'. In a later footnote she is keen to stress that in telling the story of Dickens and Ellen, she has relied 'not on Mr Wright but on the information supplied by Dickens's own daughter, Mrs Perugini' and proceeds to quote from Storey the comparison with Nelson and Lady Hamilton. She has, however, already happily copied from Wright (but without acknowledging her source) Bechhofer Roberts's apparently fictitious story about Dickens's first encounter with Ellen behind the scenes. She also embellishes it with some lively phrases of her own masquerading as quotations, as when she describes Ellen as being 'in tears at having "to show so much leg"' and Dickens as thinking her 'most attractive and a sweet little thing'. When it comes to describing the rehearsals for the Manchester production of *The Frozen Deep* she really lets her imagination rip:

> Little, fair-haired Ellen Ternan, with her sympathetic blue eyes, took up such a worshipping attitude and seemed so pathetically anxious to interpret every line and gesture according to Dickens's wishes that she completely captivated him. The rehearsals took place at Tavistock House and the more its owner coached his team, the more his infatuation for Ellen grew. Both the Miss Ternans were charming and both ran in and out of his study, but only one sat on the arm of the manager's chair, sang duets with him at the schoolroom piano and seemed, to the family, to take possession of the house.

This is followed by a version of the misdirected jewels story, which is represented as having been a wake-up call for Catherine who, 'insulted by [Dickens's] making love under her very roof to a girl of eighteen', immediately 'flared into a scene' with him. In Pope-Hennessy's version this 'scene' ends with Catherine reluctantly yielding to Dickens's request that she should demonstrate her belief in Ellen's innocence by paying a call on Mrs Ternan – then follows Kate's account, as told to Storey, about finding her distressed mother putting on her bonnet to go and visit the Ternans. Later, Pope-Hennessy incorporates into her narrative, this time *with* acknowledgement to Wright, the details from his autobiography about the evidence of the Camberwell (Peckham) rate-books and about the hearsay evidence for Dickens's visits to Ellen in Peckham. She herself does not believe 'that with Ellen Ternan Charles Dickens entered into the ideal relationship he had all his life hankered for' but deems that 'nevertheless the association must have given him some pleasure as it was kept going till his death'.

Pope-Hennessy's *Charles Dickens* was generally welcomed, though V. S. Pritchett in *The New Statesman* on 15 September was exasperated by its 'mood of chirruping equanimity'. As to *The Dickensian*, Dexter, its long-serving editor, died suddenly in 1944, having seemingly concealed from the Dickens Fellowship at large his acceptance of the truth of Storey's report of what Kate Perugini had said. His successor, Leslie C. Staples, was evidently determined to continue the official Fellowship line that the case for believing Ellen and Dickens had been lovers remained at best 'not proven'. Ralph Straus, however, whom Staples (or perhaps Dexter) had asked to review Pope-Hennessy's biography for *The Dickensian*, wrote that he 'found no difficulty whatever in accepting the fact that for some years Ellen Ternan was Dickens's mistress'. He admitted, however, that this was based on his own idea of Dickens's emotional and mental state after the Maria Beadnell disillusionment rather than on any hard evidence. As to such evidence, the new President of the Fellowship, Dickens's lawyer grandson Henry Charles Dickens, robustly declared at the 1945 Fellowship Conference that there was not enough of it 'on which to hang a cat'.

Four years later a prolific literary topographer named William Kent published his *London for the Literary Pilgrim* in which, commenting on Dickens's 'extraordinarily private' funeral in Westminster Abbey, he noted an interesting discrepancy in the *Times* report of the occasion. According to this, there were just fourteen mourners but only thirteen of them are actually named. 'The one omitted', writes Kent, 'can safely be conjectured as Ellen Ternan'. Also, in an appendix on the Dickens House Museum in Doughty Street he notes that the Dickens family, including Kate Perugini, had boycotted the opening of the Museum in 1925 on the grounds that it was a 'memorial' to Dickens, something he had expressly forbidden in his will. Referring to Kate, Kent added, 'It is ironical that this lady, so squeamish on this occasion, by the divulgence she made to a friend was to do much to damage her father's reputation as a man'. This drew an editorial protest from Staples in *The Dickensian*, showing that 'Storey-denial', so to speak, was still strong among 'loyal' Dickensians as well as sanctified memories of their much-loved Life President. Storey's evidence 'is entirely unacceptable to the Dickens Fellowship', declared Staples: 'We prefer to accept Kate Perugini's personal testimony to her love and admiration for her father, which she expressed to us on countless occasions'. He studiously ignores Kent's identification of the unnamed mourner as Ellen and, as we find from a Kent letter in a recent sales catalogue issued by specialist Dickens booksellers Jarndyce (no. 178), he was unwilling to publish a letter from Kent protesting against the exclusion of all mention of Ellen from the pages of *The Dickensian* (Straus, presumably, was too distinguished for his review to have been subjected to editorial censorship).

By the time that Kent was fluttering the Dickensian dovecots the whole debate about Dickens and Ellen had reached a kind of stalemate in Britain. Either one accepted the truth of what Wright and Storey said they had been told by Canon Benham and Kate Perugini respectively or one rejected it as completely untrustworthy, the result of misinterpretation or misunderstanding based in one case on a prurient disposition and in the other on misunderstanding and self-importance. Across the Atlantic, however, the situation was different. Edmund Wilson, a leading American critic and man of letters much influenced by Freudian theory, had become deeply interested in the revelations concerning Dickens and Ellen. As a result, he developed a startling new interpretation and critique of Dickens's life and art destined to usher in a whole new phase in the history of the Great Dickens Scandal.

CHAPTER SIX

1941–1958
Enter the scholars

Until the 1940s Dickens was very much below the academic radar in the English-speaking world. In 1948 Louis B. Frewer of the Bodleian Library referred in *The Dickensian* to 'academic, hidebound Oxford, where one mentions the name of Dickens almost in a whisper'. And indeed Oxford was still holding out against Dickens as late as 1960 when I was there as a graduate student. I wanted to make some aspect of his work the subject of my thesis and found myself being urged to find a more 'solid' topic. One of the few professional academics to devote a whole book to him before World War II was the American Edward Wagenknecht. In his so-called 'psychobiography' *The Man Charles Dickens: A Victorian Portrait* (1929) he paints Dickens in glowing colours, and although Ellen does get a mention, the idea that she and Dickens might actually have been lovers is resolutely scouted. Dickens, Wagenknecht declares, was simply not 'an amorous man'.

The situation began to change, at least outside Oxford, in the early 1940s when two leading and highly influential intellectuals, George Orwell in England and Edmund Wilson in America, each published an epoch-making essay on Dickens. In his 'Charles Dickens', published in *Inside the Whale* (1940), George Orwell was concerned with Dickens's literary art and social criticism, not with his personal life. He takes note of *This Side Idolatry* but believes that 'a writer's literary life has little or nothing to do with his private character'. The American critic Edmund Wilson, on the other hand, was deeply interested in Dickens's personal history and found him to be an eminently suitable case for Freudian treatment. In his epoch-making essay 'Dickens: the Two Scrooges', published in *The Wound and the Bow* in 1941, Wilson argued that Dickens had, as a result of his traumatic childhood experience in the blacking-factory, developed into an extraordinary mixture of fervent social reformer and rebel, or even criminal outlaw, with the latter element beginning to predominate in his later years. Having read both Wright and Storey, Wilson found Dickens's relationship with Ellen to have had an enormous impact on his art in the later novels.

Wilson misrepresents Storey's book by saying that it was based on 'interviews' with Kate Perugini, thus conferring on it a kind of authority it does not possess. He follows Wright and Kingsmill, though dismissing the latter as a minor Lytton Strachey, in finding Ellen reflected in certain major female characters in the later novels – Lucie Manette ('Dickens's dramatisation of the first hopeless phase of his love'), Estella, Bella Wilfer, Helena Landless and Rosa Budd. He repeats the Bechhofer Roberts story about Dickens's first backstage meeting with a tearfully embarrassed Ellen and even contributes a new detail to it: 'when Dickens first saw her she was hiding behind one of the properties and crying'. He also contrives to associate her with Mary Hogarth: 'she evidently appealed to that compassionate interest in young women which had made [Dickens] apotheosize Mary Hogarth'. In his account Catherine Dickens gets barely a mention ('she may have been a scold'), and Mrs Ternan and her two elder daughters vanish from the record altogether. He describes Dickens involving Ellen in his (unspecified) 'benefit performances' and casting her in roles 'which ran close enough to the real situation to offend Mrs Dickens', which seems to be another new embellishment to the story. According to Wilson, Dickens 'induced' Ellen to become his mistress after his separation from Catherine and 'set her up in an establishment of her own'. He appears to be following a hint from Hugh Kingsmill when he notes that 'it seems to be the general opinion that Ellen was neither so fascinating nor so gifted as Dickens thought her'. This is an idea that obviously sits well with what seemed by then to have become the general belief, traceable all the way back to Thomas Wright, that Dickens had, in general, a pretty wretched time of it with his young mistress. Wilson also accepts as true Kate Perugini's reported statement that Ellen bore Dickens a child who died. This leads him to speculate, as others would do after him, that this event may perhaps be reflected in Dickens's 1865 Christmas Story *Doctor Marigold*. This is the tale in which the cheapjack Marigold's beloved child dies in his arms while he has to keep up his comic patter designed to inveigle his hearers into buying his shoddy goods.

By his use of their books Wilson certainly conferred academic prestige on Wright and Storey, but he was not concerned with producing new factual evidence to feed the scandal, so there was nothing new for the Dickensians to combat. His publishers, who evidently recognised a lost cause when they saw one, declined to send a review copy to *The Dickensian*, so Walter Dexter was able to get away with simply jeering at the essay as having been written solely to make money by attacking Dickens.

Stimulated no doubt by Wilson's essay, American scholars soon began discovering new documentary evidence bearing on Dickens's relationship with Ellen. In 1943 John D. Gordan published an essay entitled 'The Secret of Dickens' Memoranda'. He had been examining in the Huntington Library in Los Angeles the memorandum that Dickens had drawn up for Wills's guidance before leaving for his American reading tour in November 1867. By means of infrared photography Gordan had been able to decipher a paragraph that had been heavily inked out, presumably by Georgina as she trawled through the file of Dickens's letters to Wills loaned to her by his great-nephew Rudolph C. Lehmann who had inherited them. This memorandum, minus the deleted paragraph, was included by Lehmann in his *Charles Dickens As Editor. Being Letters Written By Him To William Henry Wills His Sub-Editor* (1912). The deleted paragraph is headed 'Nelly' and tells Wills that Ellen will come to him if she needs help of any kind. Dickens also gives Wills the address in Florence at which she will be staying, the Villa Trollope, home of her brother-in-law Tom Trollope. The blotted-out paragraph also tells Wills that Dickens will send him a telegram immediately after arriving in America. Wills must copy its 'exact words' and send them on to Ellen in Florence as they will have 'a special meaning' for her.

Gordan also published another paragraph of this memorandum to Wills that had evidently escaped Georgina's censoring eye but that had nevertheless been tactfully suppressed by Lehmann. This tells Wills that Forster 'knows Nelly as you do, and will do anything for her if you want anything done' (meaning especially, one presumes, anything involving money). Ignorant as to what the wording of the all-important telegram was, Gordan was not able to make much of his discoveries but believed that 'even the surface meaning stirs the imagination when one thinks of the ill and aging lover and remorseful young woman who was his mistress'. Clearly, he, like Wilson, accepted the depressing account of Dickens's relationship with Ellen that Wright claimed to have been given by Benham. Gordan comments:

Dickens seems to have been in love with her youth and she with his fame and wealth. He was aware that a feeling of guilt haunted her. The memory of her affair with Dickens seems to have filled her with disgust and remorse.

Three years later Professor Franklin P. Rolfe of the University of California at Los Angeles published in the academic journal *Nineteenth Century Fiction* another very remarkable communication from Dickens to Wills of an earlier date which is also now in the Huntington Library. This was a letter of 25 October 1858 that clearly showed Dickens as already taking on the role of patron and protector of the whole Ternan family. Maria and Ellen were still working actresses in the West End and Dickens tells Wills that they were living in lodgings in Berners Street, off Oxford Street, while their mother and elder sister Fanny had gone to Florence, at his expense, in order for Fanny to 'complete a musical education'. The implication is that he had arranged these lodgings for them, having, as he told Wills, persuaded Mrs Ternan that their previous abode was unhealthy. The two young women seem to have been annoyed or alarmed or both by the (unspecified) behaviour of a policeman who Dickens suspects might have been bribed by some 'Swell' interested in Maria. He asks Wills to go and see Maria and Ellen to get the full story from them and then, armed with this information, to go to Scotland Yard with a demand that the matter be investigated.

Rolfe's professorial colleague at UCLA Ada Nisbet reprinted this letter in her *Dickens and Ellen Ternan* which appeared three years later with a six-page 'Foreword' by no less a personage than Edmund Wilson himself. Nisbet also published for the first time part of another remarkable letter which she had discovered in the Pierpont Morgan Library, New York. It was written by Dickens on 15 July 1858 to a certain Richard Smith Spofford, an American lawyer-cousin of the Ternans. Concerned, one presumes, for the family honour, Spofford had evidently written to Dickens about all the scandal that was being printed in the American press linking his name with that of a London actress named 'Miss Ternan'. Spofford naturally assumed that this referred to Fanny, she being the eldest of the Ternan sisters and therefore the only one entitled to be called 'Miss Ternan'. Nisbet quotes the paragraph in which Dickens, after some rather florid flattery of Spofford, praising his 'noble instinct' – manifested, presumably, by his refusal to believe the rumours – assures the American that 'there could not live upon this earth a man more blamelessly and openly her [i.e., Fanny's] friend than I am, or to whom her honor could be dearer than it is to me'. Nisbet rather missed a trick, however, by failing to quote the letter in full. Had she done so, Dickens would have been revealed as being somewhat economical with the truth in that he said no word to Spofford about the financial assistance he was giving to Fanny in order to make her Italian venture possible.

Nisbet had still more exciting discoveries to report, however. She had examined in the Berg Collection in the New York Public Library a small pocket diary for 1867 that had belonged to Dickens and that, to his great perturbation, he had lost during his American reading tour. Nisbet made little of this item ('only the most inconsequential single-line daily entries') till she came across something thrilling, 'hidden away in some blank pages at the back'. This was nothing less than a key to the meaning of the telegram that, as was known from Gordan's earlier discovery, Wills was to receive from Dickens as soon as he arrived in America, the 'exact words' of which Wills was immediately to copy and forward to Ellen in Florence:

Tel: all well means
you come

Tel: safe and well, means
  you don't come
To Wills. Who sends the Te. on to
  Villa Trollope
  fuori la porta S'Niccolo
  Florence

Clearly Dickens, distressed by the prospect of a six-month separation from Ellen, had hoped to bring her to America while he
was there. After all, she did have some American relatives to visit.
However, the reality of his being once again in America, as a huge
celebrity and this time giving public performances in city after
city, must have convinced him pretty quickly that it would be
simply impossible for him and Ellen to have any privacy during
his visit. The telegram that was despatched to Wills on 22
November duly read, 'Safe & well expect good letter full of
Hope'. In 1912 Lehmann had included this document without
comment in his edition as well as a still-puzzling second telegram
(not commented on by Nisbet but much speculated about since,
though *not* by the Editors of the Pilgrim Edition of Dickens's
letters) sent to Wills on 4 December: 'Tremendous success
greatest enthusiasm all well'. Can Dickens have changed his mind
and now be sending Ellen the coded message 'all well' meaning
that she *should* come to America? If so, she did not act upon it.

Nisbet had equally sensational discoveries to report from the
Huntington Library where, like Gordan, she too invoked the aid
of infrared photography to examine certain passages in Dickens's
letters to Wills from America which, like the Ellen passage in
the memorandum retrieved by Gordan, had been blacked out
and recovered by Rolfe using the same method. The first of
these, occurring in a letter of 21 November, informed Wills that
Dickens would be sending his letters to Ellen, his 'dear Girl' as
he called her, care of Wills since he did not quite know where

1 Dickens photographed by Herbert Watkins in 1858

2 Ellen Ternan about 1860

3 Catherine Dickens in later years

4 Georgina Hogarth by
Augustus Egg, about 1850

5 Georgina Hogarth
photographed in 1906

6 Sir Henry Fielding Dickens giving a reading from his father's works

7 Mr and Mrs George Wharton Robinson and their son Geoffrey (born 1879)

8 C. E. Bechhofer Roberts

9 J. W. T. Ley

He died among his children and could
have died with no better words and no
better hopes. God be thanked for it, and
may such mercy and comfort be in store
for us!

Pray give my kind regards to Margaret
and your brother.

Always yours affectionately,
CHARLES DICKENS.

And that was the last letter Dickens
wrote to his boyhood love.

(Copyright throughout the world by Christy and Moore
Reproduction in whole or in part expressly forbidden.

out of his vitality; but—almost equally
of course—it was a shock too, for all the
old Past comes out of its grave when I
think of him, and the Ghosts of a good
many years stand about his memory.

10 Illustration drawn by Pisani for *The Sunday Graphic*, 25 February 1934

11 Thomas Wright

12 Canon William Benham

13 Walter Dexter

14 Gladys Storey photographed by Bassano in 1939

15 Kate Perugini in 1923 drawn by Gladys Storey

16 Kate Perugini as Hon. Life President of the Dickens Fellowship

17 Edgar Johnson on the cover of *The Saturday Evening Post*, 10 January 1953

18 Ada Nisbet

19 Cover of *Dickens and the Scandalmongers*, 1965

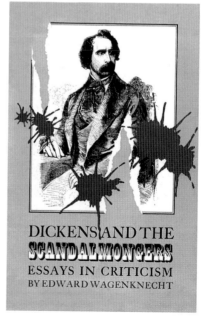

DICKENS AND THE
SCANDALMONGERS
ESSAYS IN CRITICISM
BY EDWARD WAGENKNECHT

20 Sir Felix Aylmer

21 William J. Carlton

Felix Aylmer

| 13 | S | Oxf. T. ends | To sl: at 10.25. at Sl: at 2½ Arrival

DICKENS
INCOGNITO

| 20 | S | ̶[̶Alphege] To off from Sl: at 11.40 [x1 050.] To 9. H.

*Who, where and why
was Mr Tringham?*

*And was his Christian name
John, Charles, Francis or Thomas?*

22 Cover of *Dickens Incognito* (1959)

23 Katharine M. Longley holding a portrait of Ellen Ternan

24 Cartoon drawn by Richard Willson to accompany a review of *The Invisible Woman* in *The Sunday Times*, 4 November 1990

she would be. She would let Wills know where to send them on to her. Nisbet then prints the retrieved texts of ten blacked-out passages from Dickens sent to Wills between 3 December 1867 and 17 April 1868, all mentioning that a letter for Ellen (variously referred to as 'my dear girl', 'my Darling', 'my dear Patient') was enclosed. One, written on Christmas Eve, included the words, 'I would give £3,000 down (and think it cheap) if you could forward *me*, for four and twenty hours only, instead of the letter'.

Aware that the discovery of proof positive that Ellen bore Dickens a child was (as it still remains) the Golden Fleece for Dickens biographers, Nisbet pauses over the strange phrase 'my dear Patient', used with reference to Ellen in a letter of 21 February 1868. Might this not suggest that Ellen was at this time pregnant? This could hardly have been the case, however, for Dickens had been using this name for Ellen from shortly after the Staplehurst accident, in which, it would seem, she suffered some injury, and, as Nisbet's research showed, he continued to do so until the end of his life. She quotes several other letters to Wills dating from 12 July 1865 to 23 January 1870 in all of which Dickens refers to Ellen as 'the Patient'. Of course all of these references had also been carefully blacked out by Georgina or Lehmann himself before he began preparing Dickens's letters to Wills for publication in *Charles Dickens as Editor*.

Nisbet also draws attention to two passages in earlier letters from Dickens to Wills, written from Doncaster on 17 and 20 September 1857, that had not been blacked out but just silently omitted by Lehmann. In the first Dickens wrote:

> But Lord bless you, the strongest parts of your present correspondent's heart are made up of weaknesses, and he just come here at all (if you knew it) along of his Richard Wardour! Guess *that* riddle, Mr. Wills!

And in the second:

> I am going to take the little – riddle – into the country this
> morning; and I answer your letter briefly before starting. . . . so
> let the riddle and the riddler go their own wild way, and no
> harm come of it!

Nisbet notes the allusion to Wardour, Dickens's role in *The
Frozen Deep*, that of an older man passionately in love with a
younger woman who does not return his love, and speculates
that 'a close reading' of the play 'would reveal many lines which
take on a special meaning when one remembers the dragon's
teeth being sown during those Manchester rehearsals'. In her last
chapter she defends what she calls her 'decanonization' of
Dickens by arguing that knowing about his passion for Ellen
should help us to a deeper and richer understanding of his later
work as the product of what she calls 'the spiritual tragedy of his
later years'. She ends by publishing for the first time a sentence
from a since much-quoted passage in Dickens's letter to Georgina
of 1 February 1863 in which he tells her how moved he has
been by a production of Gounod's *Faust* at the Paris Opera: 'It
affected me so and sounded in my ears so like a mournful echo
of things that lie in my own heart'. Here again, she missed a trick
by not quoting the letter at greater length as Edgar Johnson does
in his contemporaneous biography. Had she done so, her readers
would have been made aware of the piquant detail that the point
in the opera at which Dickens broke down was the one at which
the heroine Marguerite is seduced by the superb jewels left for
her as bait by Faust and Mephistopheles.

Nisbet's book was somewhat wearily reviewed in *The Times
Literary Supplement* by Bernard Darwin on 3 July 1953. He
thought the 'now well-worn subject of the relations between
Dickens and Ellen Ternan' was 'not a very pleasant one' and hoped

that one day public attention would turn fully back to the great Dickens novels. He somewhat oddly thought the use of infrared photography rather 'unsportsmanlike' but conceded that it might perhaps be justified if it helped to settle this distracting controversy once and for all. He also regretted that in her combative remarks about the detractors of Wright, Storey and others, Nisbet showed 'too eager a desire to dethrone Dickens from the pinnacle of Victorian morality on which he has been unwisely placed', but he did believe that she had settled beyond reasonable doubt the question about the nature of Dickens's relationship with Ellen. Two days later V. S. Pritchett's review appeared in *The New Statesman*. Nisbet, he believed, was simply adding some corroborative details to what had already been abundantly shown by Wright and Storey, i.e., that Ellen was indeed Dickens's mistress, though 'some last-ditch Dickensians still cling to Dickens's passionately virtuous disclaimer that the affair was merely the platonic interest of a man of 45 for a pretty girl of 18'. In the course of his characteristically stimulating review, Pritchett gives his own, non-moralising, view of the relationship: 'A self-willed man is in love with a rather cool, prim, frightened, kittenish, unimaginative girl who is likely to exploit the power her youth gives over him.'

1952 also saw the publication of the most substantial and ambitious biography of Dickens to appear since Forster's. Swiftly labelled 'definitive', it remained unchallenged for over thirty years. *Charles Dickens: His Tragedy and Triumph* was written by Professor Edgar Johnson of the City College of New York and was based on many years of exhaustive research. It is very much, as its title suggests, a biography with a thesis. That thesis is adumbrated in the first words of the Preface (which also introduce us to Johnson's somewhat bravura style):

Charles Dickens . . . is a titan of literature, and his own moving life-story, with its radiances of laughter, its conquests of genius, and its dark and fateful drift towards disillusion even in the midst of universal acclaim, epitomizes hardly less powerfully than his works the mingled comedy and tragedy of the human struggle.

Johnson's take on Dickens's relationship with Ellen when he reaches that period of the biography is, in fact, very much the same as Thomas Wright's. He finds the story about Dickens's first meeting with her when she was distressed by the scantiness of her costume 'rather dubious', but suggests that if it did really happen it may have been merely a ploy to gain Dickens's attention: 'She might, of course, have felt she would be more interesting to a great author if discovered in a role of outraged modesty and prettily timorous purity'. He enlivens the imagined context of the 1858 letter to Wills about the Berners Street policeman and the Ternan sisters (above, p. 114) by saying that they had 'been subjected to indecent persecution' by the man, which makes him sound more like a stalker than a possible pander. Generally, Johnson writes very much under the influence of Edmund Wilson and like him, and like Wright before Wilson, he reads somewhat crudely from the later novels back into Dickens's later life. He writes that by 1862, for example, 'the desperate infatuation mirrored in Pip's obsession with Estella was gnawing with ever sharper fangs into his [Dickens's] heart'. To Johnson the reason for this seems 'evident' in that 'Ellen was unresponsive to his need and cold to his emotion'. In Johnson's story of the relationship Ellen makes Dickens wait rather longer for her favours than he has to in Wright's version of events. We remember that according to Wright (citing Benham), 'No great while after the separation . . . Dickens prevailed upon Miss Ternan to become his mistress; but she gave herself reluctantly'. Johnson, however, believes for some reason – presumably the vividness of Dickens's description of Pip's sufferings in *Great*

Expectations – that this probably happened rather later. Although, he writes, there is 'no undeniable evidence' (in point of fact, there is no *evidence* at all), he thinks it 'not unlikely that either now [in Paris in January 1863] or during the previous period of almost a month in England, Ellen's obduracy had at last given way', but believes that her surrender brought Dickens 'little of that shining ecstasy with which throbbing imagination conceives the world will be transformed by triumphant love'.

Johnson had examined Dickens's 1867 pocket-diary in the Berg Collection independently of Nisbet (though at work at the same time, they do not seem to have liaised over their researches into Dickens's life) and had also found the code for the tele-grams, which was not 'hidden away in some blank pages at the back' as reported by Nisbet but written where it belongs, oppo-site the calendar for November. Like Nisbet, he quotes the entry as well as the same passages from Dickens's 1867 memorandum to Wills that were suppressed by Lehmann. He quotes copiously from Kate Perugini as reported by Storey and expresses the opinion that Dickens's relationship with Ellen was an unhappy one: 'There is reason for believing that Dickens had won Ellen against her will, wearing down her resistance by sheer force of desperate determination, and that her conscience never ceased to reproach her'. He thus accepts the Wright version, with the one variant as regards timing already noted. He does, however, produce some new evidence, in addition to that being contem-poraneously published by Nisbet, which could be said to strengthen the basic assumption that Dickens and Ellen were lovers. He is able, for example, to provide a fuller text of Dickens's letter to the Station Master at Charing Cross on 12 June 1865 following the Staplehurst accident, the letter about a lady who had been travelling in his carriage and who in being rescued had lost some gold trinkets – he had, wrote Dickens, promised to make enquiries on her behalf. As we have seen, only a summary of, and brief extract from, this letter (both taken from a sale-catalogue) had appeared in the Nonesuch Letters, but Johnson, having tracked down the actual letter, can now quote Dickens's detailed description of the lost trinkets: 'a gold watch-chain with a smaller gold watch-chain attached, a bundle of charms, a gold watch-key, and a gold seal engraved "Ellen"'. It was hardly necessary, one might think, for him to defend in a footnote his belief that the 'Ellen' in question must have been Ellen: '. . . it is obviously beyond all likelihood that chance would have placed in the same compartment with him another lady of the same Christian name in whose behalf he would be likely to make the enquiry'. It is strange, though, that it did not seem to occur to him to suggest that the unnamed old lady travelling in the same compartment with Dickens and Ellen and sitting opposite to them must surely have been Mrs Ternan.

Johnson takes from Wright the details regarding Ellen's presumed residence from 1867 on in Windsor Lodge, Peckham. He deals briskly with Dickens's 'magic circle' letter to Frances Elliot of 4 July 1867 (see above, p. 95). Its meaning is, he thinks, 'perfectly clear'. Elliot has learned about Dickens's affair with Ellen and has suggested meeting her, a request that Dickens 'out of regard for Ellen's feelings . . . felt obliged to reject'. Johnson is the first person, however, to have investigated Dickens's financial records in the archives of his bankers Coutts & Co. and in a long footnote to chapter 2 of Part 10 of his biography he records that between 17 October 1866 and 14 January 1867 Dickens made out six cheques totalling £127.10 to 'N Trust' (he pertinently reminds us that Dickens often referred to Ellen as 'N'). He also notes a cheque for £150 paid to 'Wills Trust' on 7 November 1867 and two very large cheques paid to Wills while Dickens was in America (£1,000 on 27 January 1868 and £1,100 on 2 March 1868) and comments, 'In view of Dickens' parting memorandum to Wills about Ellen, and Dickens' decision not to have her join him in America, the reader may give these payments totalling £2,250 what significance he wishes'. It seems clear that Johnson himself, not unreasonably, considers that these financial records strongly suggest that Ellen was indeed Dickens's mistress, or was at least financially dependent on him.

She pretty much vanishes from Johnson's narrative after Dickens's American reading tour. By this time, Johnson believes, Dickens was emotionally exhausted and disillusioned, and 'had ceased to care what happened to him'. While he concedes that 'There is no direct evidence of what part Ellen played in his unhappiness', he believes 'there can be no doubt that in some way she, too, failed his need'. For indirect evidence he turns back to the old game of inferring various traits of Ellen's character and behaviour from selected female characters in the later novels. Was she perhaps a Bella Wilfer who failed to reform but stayed mercenary so that Dickens's love for her was 'shot through with a disillusioned bitterness that only a wraith like the memory of Mary Hogarth need not fear'? As for Dickens's leaving her a legacy in his will, this to Johnson 'reveals an odd blindness, carelessness, or indifference – surely one of the three – to the certainty that her name would be coupled with his when the contents of the will became known'.

The year 1952 thus saw two industrious American scholars, working independently but both strongly influenced by Edmund Wilson, bringing to light a great deal of new circumstantial evidence pointing towards the fact that Dickens and Ellen had indeed been lovers just as Thomas Wright had claimed. In the same year an English scholar K. J. Fielding published in the journal *Nineteenth Century Fiction* some legal documents he had discovered that dramatically illustrate the prevalence of the more sinister of the two main scandals that swirled about Dickens in 1858. This was the one about his relationship with Georgina that Thackeray had been so eager to deny. A Glaswegian well-wisher wrote to warn Dickens that the editor of a local newspaper, Colin Rae Brown, was going about the city, in which Dickens had just been giving some hugely successful readings, saying that he was 'the outcry of London' and asserting that his 'sister-in-law had had three children by him'. Dickens, given the highly damaging nature of the charge, had no option but to instruct his lawyers to inform Rae Brown that they would be instituting libel proceedings against him. Fortunately, Rae Brown immediately backed down, asserting that he had been gravely misreported, and no action needed to be taken.

The following year, in two successive issues of *The Sunday Times* (8 and 15 March, 1953), the former Lord Chancellor Earl Jowitt scrutinised from a lawyer's viewpoint all the new evidence regarding Dickens's relationship with Ellen that had been unearthed by Johnson and Nisbet, and looked back also over the earlier evidence provided by Wright and Storey. He found the testimony of these last two witnesses unsatisfactory in various respects, especially Storey's report that Kate Perugini had said Ellen had borne Dickens a child that had died:

> This fact – if fact it be – is plainly outside Mrs Perugini's personal knowledge, and we are given no clue as to the source from which Mrs Perugini derived her information. I cannot under the circumstances think it right to attach any importance to this statement which is entirely uncorroborated from any other source.

He did, however, find that Dickens's 1867 letter to Frances Elliot showed conclusively that 'there was some secret' concerning Dickens's relationship with Ellen and he went on to note 'the intensity of passion' shown in Dickens's references to Ellen contained in his letters to Wills from America. This, Jowitt wrote, led him to the 'safe conclusion' that 'by the year 1867, and probably some years earlier' Ellen had indeed become Dickens's mistress. He added as a sort of rider to his judgment that this finding in no way diminished his 'profound respect and gratitude for the man' or his admiration and love for his works. This must have softened the blow that his judgment would have given to those devoted Dickensians who still clung to the idea of their hero's purity. As to the Dickens Fellowship in general, its members' overall acceptance of Jowitt's judgment would seem to have been signalled by their election of him later in the year to the office of President, the highest honour the society could confer.

The Sunday Times for 22 March included a crop of letters responding to Jowitt's articles. Sir Sydney Cockerell, Curator of the Fitzwilliam Museum, Cambridge, wrote to say that as a boy in Margate he had heard Ellen give brilliant recitals of the *Christmas Carol*. He had also met Mamie Dickens and Georgina Hogarth as guests of the Robinsons and remembered that they were 'evidently on the best of terms' with their hosts. As to the possibility that Ellen had perhaps been Dickens's mistress, Sir Sydney takes a bluff, man of the world line: 'surely so frequent a situation is being unduly magnified'. Gladys Storey wrote to protest against Jowitt's comment that she had got the Peckham address from Wright rather than direct from Kate Perugini as stated in her book. And a letter from a Mr H. J. Chilton supplied some further relevant information about Mrs Goldring. She had worked in Peckham for his grandmother as well as for 'Mr Tringham' and it was remembered in his family that she had had no idea of Mr Tringham's true identity until she saw a picture of Dickens in a newspaper whereupon she had exclaimed, 'Well, if it isn't the Master!'

Five years later Professor Arthur A. Adrian of Case Western Reserve University, Ohio, published his *Georgina Hogarth and the Dickens Circle*. He paints a highly favourable portrait of

Georgina as having been very much the woman described by Dickens in his will and closely follows Wright and Johnson in his discussion of Dickens and Ellen. He writes with great confidence about their feelings but leaves himself some wriggle-room through his liberal use of words and phrases like 'must have', 'perhaps', 'apparently' and 'if':

> Georgina must have suspected, perhaps known, that in the Ellen Ternan affair Dickens had only exchanged one heartache for another. Ellen, though dazzled by the older man's fame, . . . apparently did not respond with the whole-souled devotion he craved. Dickens was no libertine . . . . Ellen, if she had submitted to his advances after the separation, seems to have done so coldly and with a worried sense of guilt. Such a capitulation could only have tormented Dickens with a still keener sense of his own guilt.

Adrian did, however, unearth some notable fragments of indirect evidence relative to Dickens's relationship with Ellen from his examination at the Massachusetts Historical Society of the diary kept by Annie Fields, the wife of Dickens's American publisher, James T. Fields. The Fieldses became intimate friends of Dickens during his gruelling American readings tour and were also his hosts on some occasions. Annie herself became romantically devoted to him. When he is concerned that news about his ill-health may reach and alarm his loved ones in England, Annie writes, 'Ah! What a mystery these ties of love are – such pain, such ineffable happiness – the only happiness'. This does not sound as though she is thinking of Dickens's emotional ties with Georgina or with his daughters. Later, meditating on Dickens's 'strange lot', Annie writes, 'May his mistakes be expiated', without any comment on the nature of the 'mistakes' to which she is referring, but probably meaning his relationship with

Ellen. And in her diary for 2 May 1868, the day Dickens's homeward-bound ship docked in Liverpool, she writes: 'I cannot help rehearsing in my mind the intense joy of his beloved. It is too much to face, even in one's imagination – and too sacred. Yet I know today to be the day and these hours, *his hours*. Tomorrow Gad's Hill.' Adrian notes that the 'beloved' reference cannot be to Georgina, who, Annie knew, was not going to meet him off the boat in Liverpool but to wait for him at Gad's Hill with Mamie, so that Annie can have been referring only to Ellen. It seems unlikely that, if she had believed Dickens and Ellen were lovers in the physical sense, she would have used a term like 'sacred'. A later passage from her diary, also cited by Adrian, supports this idea. Writing in December 1872 when Christmas makes her think especially of Dickens, she records that she heard 'quite accidentally . . . the other day of N.T. being in Rome' and then adds: 'I feel the bond there is between us. She must feel it too. I wonder if we shall ever meet.' The 'bond' Annie mentions must surely refer to the love that both she and Ellen had for Dickens, with Annie assuming that Ellen's had of necessity to be as sublimated as her own.

Adrian was the last of the professional scholars who made significant discoveries about Dickens's relations with Ellen during the 1950s. In the next stage of the great Dickens scandal the leading figures were not academics but a distinguished actor, an actor-manager and theatre historian, and a retired international civil servant. Between them they were responsible for a number of significant new discoveries as well as, in the case of the first of them, the brief trajectory of a spectacular red herring.

CHAPTER SEVEN

1959–1966
The amateur contribution

From Dickens's pocket diary for 1867 in the New York Public Library Professor Ada Nisbet had gleaned some dramatic new information about his relations with Ellen Ternan. But the tiny book proved to have still more startling secrets to reveal, as was shown by the eminent English actor and long-time Dickens buff Felix Aylmer in his *Dickens Incognito* published in 1959. Aylmer had examined the diary paying close attention to the minuscule daily entries that Nisbet had passed over as 'inconsequential'. Quickly recognising that they were abbreviations mainly relating to journeys, Aylmer noted the regular recurrence of 'Sl.' as a destination, point of departure or location. Frequently recurring also were the words 'to off:' which he sensibly interpreted as 'to office', meaning the office of Dickens's journal *All the Year Round* in Wellington Street, Strand. He noted that Dickens would often record having gone 'to off:' from 'W' or 'P'. Among other journeys noted were 'To D from Wat. (for Sl.)' and 'To W from V'. Aylmer, familiar as he was with the topography of the area, soon worked out that 'Sl.' must stand for Slough, then in Buckinghamshire, just two miles from Windsor, and in 1867 still a small country village, very unlike the large manufacturing town we know today. Aylmer knew that Slough could be reached (as it still can be) by a direct train from Paddington Station, the London terminus of what was then the Great Western Railway. An alternative route would be to travel to Windsor from either Waterloo or Victoria, the London termini of what was then the London and South Western Railway. From Windsor it is a short walk to Slough or for a longer walk, which in 1867 would have been an attractively rural one, Dickens could have alighted at Datchet, the stop before Windsor.

Curious to find other evidence connecting Dickens with Slough, Aylmer on his return to England examined the 1867 rate-books of Upton-cum-Chalvey, the district to which Slough then belonged for rating purposes. He found no trace of a Charles Dickens but did, to his great excitement, discover that a certain 'John Tringham', who became 'Charles Tringham' after the first quarter, was listed as paying rates on a house in Slough from January 1866 to June 1867. Aylmer's excitement stemmed from his remembering that 'Charles Tringham' (originally 'Francis Turnham', then 'Thomas Turnham' altered to 'Thomas Tringham') had been the Dickens alias discovered in the Nunhead rate-books by Thomas Wright back in 1936, enabling him, as he thought, to prove that Dickens had maintained an establishment for Ellen in Peckham from July 1867 until his death. Aylmer was also shown two local newspaper accounts describing a fire in Slough High Street in 1889 that had burned down a house named Elizabeth Cottage and both mentioned that Dickens had lodged there for some time. From this it seems fairly clear that the true identity of 'Mr Tringham' was well known in Slough and, nine years after the publication of *Dickens Incognito*, a remarkable fragment of supporting evidence for this idea came from an unexpected quarter, a small town to the north of Auckland, New Zealand. A ninety-one-year-old inhabitant,

Gerald Dunn, wishing to dispose of some Dickens books, contacted Professor J. C. Reid of the University of Auckland whom he knew to have an interest in the subject. In his letter Mr Dunn mentioned that his father, 'who worked in the vicinity of London', had told him that he had 'worked for Dickens who was known as Tringham'. Reporting this in *The Dickensian* in 1968, Professor Reid wrote that, on investigating the matter, he had ascertained that Mr Dunn's father had been born in Slough in 1844 and had been by trade a jobbing carpenter. Also, in 'about 1866', eight years or so before he emigrated to New Zealand, Dunn senior had more than once carried out carpentry work for a Mr Tringham at a house on Slough High Street, and had been told by neighbours that Mr Tringham was, in fact, the famous novelist Charles Dickens – not very 'incognito', therefore.

In his book Aylmer notes that the most frequent initial clearly standing for a person rather than a place that features in Dickens's pocket diary during the six months of 1867 that 'Mr Tringham' was still renting Elizabeth Cottage was 'N', his usual abbreviation for Ellen. The next most frequent is 'M', who is several times noted as accompanying 'N', and Aylmer deduces that this must be Ellen's sister Maria, or it might possibly be Mrs Ternan with 'M' standing for 'Mother', though, as he admits, it is highly unlikely that Dickens would have thought of her as 'Mother'. Moreover, for the whole of these six months Mrs Ternan was professionally engaged at the Lyceum Theatre in London where the manager and leading actor was Dickens's friend Charles Fechter. Aylmer believes that she would not, in any case, have been very happy about Ellen keeping house for Dickens and would therefore have been a reluctant visitor to Elizabeth Cottage. He was probably right not to canvass a third candidate, Mamie Dickens, who, together with her Aunt Georgina, remained friendly with Ellen even after Dickens's death, since Mamie very much had her own circle of friends in

Hampshire and elsewhere. He assumes that, since Ellen was evidently located in Slough during this period, she must also have lived in Elizabeth Cottage. This leads him into some detailed speculation about the number and allocation of bedrooms in the cottage and about how 'the assurance of a blameless *ménage*' must somehow have been impressed upon Ellen's 'attached woman servant' whom Ley had quoted but not named as testifying to the purity of Ellen's relationship with Dickens in *The Dickensian* in 1937 (see above, p. 94).

By the time he has given Dickens a study in addition to a separate bedroom, and provided rooms for Ellen, visitors like Maria, and a servant, Aylmer recognises that 'the cottage must have been pretty full', so that 'the addition of Mrs Ternan as well would have meant a squeeze'. It does not seem to have occurred to him that an immense local scandal would surely have been caused by such a *ménage* and that this scandal would certainly have spread way beyond Slough. A young single woman living alone (apart from occasional visits by her sister) frequently receiving as a house guest a man who is not only unrelated to her but is none other than the famous Charles Dickens, for many years now estranged from his wife, would in itself have been scandalous enough, but it might also, if Ellen's real name was at all known, have prompted some to remember that it had been unpleasantly linked with Dickens's in metropolitan gossip at the time of his separation from his wife. Aylmer, proceeding imperturbably on the assumption that it *was* a joint establishment, merely wonders why it took nine years for Dickens to get around to setting Ellen up in a 'joint household' of their own rather than one like the Houghton Place establishment which was presided over by Mrs Ternan. He writes:

In the calendar of passion nine years is an age, and domestic arrangements which had been accepted for so long would surely have survived the four years that remained of his life if there had not been some very powerful reason for changing them.

The reason, Aylmer believes, lay in another secret that he had unearthed in the diary. Struck by the entry for 13 April 1867, 'To Sl: at 10.25. at Sl.: at 2 1/2. Arrival', he convinces himself that the last word must refer to the birth of a baby. It was, he believes, the expectation of this event that could well have been the 'very powerful reason' for this belated establishment of a joint household.

Before following Aylmer in his ill-fated pursuit of this putative infant, we should note his other great discovery. This relates to various entries in the diary between 25 March and 18 July 1867 which, as he shows, seem to document Ellen's move to Windsor Lodge, Linden Grove, Nunhead (next door to Peckham), the address to which Wright had traced her. The entry for 25 March reads, 'At Sl: Office. Houses', which, as Aylmer plausibly suggests, seems to indicate a meeting to look at house-agents' lists. Two days later comes this entry: 'Meet for houses at 12 ½. To Peckm.' Aylmer believes that Dickens and Ellen must have quickly settled on which house to take, because no further references to the subject appear until Friday 21 June on which day Dickens travelled up to town from 'G.H.' (= Gad's Hill), dined at the Athenaeum, and then went 'To temporary P' (the words '1st day' follow the P). Evidently, he had arranged some temporary lodging in the Peckham area – perhaps in the lodging-house in Hatcham that Thomas Wright later discovered he had been using on and off for some years – while Windsor Lodge was being got ready for Ellen. The entry for 22 June reads: 'At P. Long wait for N. at house'. On the 24th he is again at 'P (tem)' and yet again on the 26th, when he also notes, 'Finish Silverman, in Linden [i.e., Linden Grove]'. 'Silverman' is the story 'George

Silverman's Explanation' that he had agreed, for a very substantial fee, to write for serialisation in *The Atlantic Monthly*. Aylmer notes that 'P (tem)' disappears after this, but Dickens does make a distinction in later entries between 'P' and 'P(N)', suggesting that 'he still retained rooms outside [Windsor Lodge] for working in'. It could also be, presumably, that he slept at these rooms too so as not to bring scandal upon the head of the young mistress of Windsor Lodge. Such a hypothesis would, however, conflict with his former employee Mrs Goldring's statement, first quoted by Wright and now again by Aylmer, about Dickens's having 'lived *sub rosa* at Linden Grove, Nunhead, S.E.'.

Convinced that the entry for 13 April 1867, 'Arrival', meant the birth of a baby, Aylmer went to Somerset House to check the register of births for that day and was intrigued to discover that a child called Francis Charles Tringham was registered as having been born at the General Lying-in Hospital in York Road, London, on 10 May 1867. He became still more intrigued when he checked the Hospital's records and found no such birth recorded. Further investigation and cogitation convinced him that the Somerset House certificate was one supplied by Dickens and Ellen and that it carried 'hints of Dickens in nearly every detail'. The parents Francis Tringham, a 'housepainter journeyman', and his wife Elizabeth were recorded as living at what would seem to have been in 1867 a non-existent address. Aylmer built up a theory that Dickens and Ellen, wishing to save their child from the stigma of illegitimacy (as suffered by Esther Summerson, the heroine of *Bleak House*), had arranged for the Tringhams, presumably for some financial reward, not just to adopt the boy but to pass him off as their own child who had been born to Elizabeth Tringham on 10 May just as stated in the forged certificate. Aylmer believes that Dickens and Ellen's humane desire to spare their love-child suffering from the stain of bastardy was the reason why Ellen did not 'simply retire to some quiet spot in Europe to have her child' (as later versions of the love-child story would have her do). Other diary entries are interpreted by Aylmer in a way that supports his thesis. Given that Dickens seems to have received no visitors in Slough, might not the one exception, his confidential man of business W. H. Wills who visited on 19 April, have been for the purpose of Wills standing as godfather to the child at a private christening ceremony? Also, might not the fact that Ellen is noted as accompanying him to the Lyceum Theatre on 9 May be connected with the fact that Francis Charles Tringham was supposedly born the next day? Ellen would thus have had a perfect alibi in case of any attempt being made to connect her with the birth of Francis Charles.

In his 'Postscript' Aylmer recalls Mrs Mackie's words as reported by Wright, 'There were children', and Kate Perugini's words reported by Storey, 'There was a child but it died'. He then speculates, pretty freely, about possible siblings, short-lived or otherwise, for Francis Charles and concludes by playing the old game of interpreting the character of Ellen who, he notes, remains a 'shadowy figure' and of charting the history of her relationship with Dickens through Dickens's depiction of certain leading female characters in the later novels – the 'usual suspects', one might call them. The depiction of Bella Wilfer's change of heart in *Our Mutual Friend* leads Aylmer to date Ellen's final surrender to Dickens's ardour 'either before *Our Mutual Friend* was begun or early in 1865'. And he trusts Pope-Hennessy's 'feminine instinct' in identifying Rosa Budd in *Edwin Drood* as Dickens's final portrait of Ellen as a charming young woman who is 'babyish and wilful' but who will outgrow these faults as she matures. His final verdict is that Dickens's alleged relationship with Ellen is not 'a happy romance to contemplate', but he believes that its discomforts probably resulted more from the pressures of contemporary social conditions than from the characters or behaviour of the lovers themselves.

A much condensed version of *Dickens Incognito* was published in *The Sunday Times* on 5 December 1959 and was followed a week later by a letter from Graham Storey, one of the editors of the projected grand new Pilgrim Edition of Dickens's Letters. Storey completely demolishes Aylmer's theory that Francis Charles Tringham was the love-child of Dickens and Ellen. He had followed Aylmer to the General Lying-in Hospital in York Road and had quickly found the record of Francis Tringham's birth that had been unaccountably overlooked by Aylmer as well as other evidence that the birth certificate was completely genuine. A rueful letter from Aylmer appeared below Storey's, perforce withdrawing his contention that Francis Charles Tringham was the son of Dickens and Ellen but still clinging to his belief that there *was* a son who had 'to be provided with an apparently normal birth certificate' and that 'by duplication of names it was made possible for him in future life to make use of a registration actually effected for someone else'. There is evidence in his papers now in the Charles Dickens Museum that Aylmer did for a while pursue at least one other possible candidate for this presumed son.

In his book Aylmer acknowledges help received on a particular point from the noted actor-manager and theatre historian Malcolm Morley, this help being based on information Morley himself had received from Ellen's married daughter Gladys Reece. Reece also seems to have given Morley a great deal of help, including access to family photographs and other material, with his series of ten articles chronicling the private and professional histories of the Ternan family, published in *The Dickensian* between 1958 and 1961. In this series called 'The Theatrical Ternans' Morley gives a vast amount of detailed, but unfortunately undocumented as published, information about the domestic history and stage careers of the Ternan family, derived from contemporary sources. He begins with Ellen's maternal grandparents, John and Maria Jarman, originally of the Theatre Royal, York. He describes how Fanny, their highly talented daughter and the future mother of Ellen, won considerable acclaim for herself on the stage before her marriage to a turbulent Irish tragedian named Thomas Lawless Ternan in 1834. He traces the ups and downs of the couple's subsequent career, on both sides of the Atlantic, and records the births of their three daughters as well as the dates of the children's respective stage débuts. Ellen's took place in 1842 when she was three years old, playing a child in an old war-horse of the nineteenth-century British theatrical repertoire, *The Stranger*. Morley reveals the tragedy that befell the family when Ternan, too ill to continue working, had to be confined in a mental home in Bethnal Green where in 1846, according to Morley, he killed himself 'in a fit of despair' (the suicide allegation later turned out to be erroneous). Morley also records the courage and determination of his widow in maintaining her place almost in the front rank of contemporary actresses whilst keeping the family together, educating her three daughters and cultivating their talents. He describes the eldest, the musically gifted Fanny, as the cleverest of the sisters, Maria the second daughter as the liveliest and most entertaining, and Ellen the youngest as 'more sensitive, more reserved' but 'possessed of sympathy and understanding' that caused her to 'respond freely to the joys and sorrows of others'. Here, in this description of her mother as in many other places in the series, one can sense the presence of Ellen's daughter looking over Morley's shoulder as he writes.

Morley tells the story, attributing it to Wright but querying its provenance, of Dickens finding Ellen in tears behind the scenes at the Haymarket and puts a special gloss on it. 'Wearing the abbreviated costume would have been no ordeal to her sisters', he writes: 'Ellen, however, was the least theatrical of the Ternans and shrank all her life from the publicity of the stage'. This was written, no doubt, in the consciousness that he would later be recording Ellen's retirement from the stage at the age of twenty, less than eighteen months after meeting Dickens, and that he would need to describe it in such a way as not to make the one event seem the direct result of the other. Throughout the series he strives hard to steer clear of scandal, but nevertheless it is he who reveals that Mrs Ternan, Maria and Ellen were all acting at the theatre in Doncaster in Races Week, September 1857, when Dickens and Wilkie Collins were also there, ostensibly to get copy for 'The Lazy Tour of Two Idle Apprentices' serial that they were writing jointly for *Household Words*. Morley seeks to present this highly suggestive fact in as non-committal a way as possible. He notes that Dickens and Collins, whose presence and movements were reported in the local press, do not seem, according to that source, to have attended the theatre on the one night they were there when Maria and Ellen were both performing. He does think it likely, however, that the Ternans might have joined forces with Dickens and Collins to go and watch the St. Leger horse-race and that 'the friendship that sprung up between Dickens and the [Ternan] family might have ripened during the time he spent there [in Doncaster]'. We can be pretty sure, I think, judging from his treatment of William Kent (see above, p. 108), that short shrift would have been given by Leslie Staples, then editing *The Dickensian*, to any sharp-eyed reader who might have suggested a connection between this new information about Ellen's presence in Doncaster in September 1857 and the 'little riddle' jokes in Dickens's letters from there to Wills as revealed by Nisbet, or the ecstatic description in chapter 5 of 'The Lazy Tour' of the golden-haired owner of 'a pair of little lilac gloves' and a 'winning little bonnet' who, watching the race, had captured the heart of 'Mr Goodchild', as Dickens calls himself in the 'Tour'.

In Morley's narrative Dickens is made to figure as a kindly and generous friend of the Ternan family, a sort of 'fairy godfather' (to borrow a splendidly apt phrase from a distinguished modern Dickens scholar, Rosemary Bodenheimer). He suggests that Fanny, who was ambitious to become a great singer, should spend two years abroad studying opera-singing in Italy and, 'knowing the financial strain it would be on the family resources', offers to help with the expenses. Morley goes on to detail the busy metropolitan stage careers of Maria and Ellen in 1858 and the move from the family's home in Park Cottage, Canonbury, to Berners Street, but omits to say that this move was made at Dickens's suggestion, he having, as he told Wills in the 'policeman' letter (see above, p. 114), persuaded Mrs Ternan that Park Cottage was 'unwholesome'. Morley relates the incident of the intrusive policeman, also the family's further move to 2 Houghton Place on Mrs Ternan's return from Italy, but says nothing, of course, about the economic basis of this latter move. He describes Maria's triumphs in a succession of comedy roles while continuing to build up the picture of Ellen as a reluctant actress, 'decorative' and with 'a pleasant voice', but never giving herself entirely to any of the (minor) parts she was playing. Finally, in August 1859, she resolves to renounce the theatre altogether, the implication being that she had decided it was not the career for her. With his eye on Ellen's daughter, no doubt, Morley comments, 'The only kindred employment that was to occupy her mind in the future was the teaching of elocution and . . . giving instruction in the dramatic poets'.

Morley cites Francesco Berger's reported memories of card-playing and duet-singing evenings with Mrs Ternan, Ellen and Dickens at Houghton Place which have only very recently been shown to be suspect (see below, p. 184). After this, however, Ellen disappears from his narrative altogether while he goes into consid-erable detail about the careers of Fanny and Maria. She is suddenly mentioned again many pages later as having visited Gad's Hill and been introduced to Georgina, 'thus beginning an enduring friendship between the two'. Then comes the account of the Staplehurst accident with no comment whatever on the (on the face of it) interesting fact that Ellen and Dickens were returning from France together. He is, however, the first person to make the obvious surmise that the old lady in the carriage with Dickens and Ellen must have been her mother. No doubt he thought this helped to confer respectability on the travelling party. From Staplehurst he moves quickly on to Fanny's marriage with Tom Trollope and Maria's with an Oxford brewer, William Taylor.

In Part VIII Morley returns to Mrs Ternan and Ellen. He describes them as living together at an unspecified address in Slough and now the difficulty he is working under becomes obvious. On the one hand, he wants to make use of Aylmer's discoveries about Elizabeth Cottage but, on the other, he needs to keep Gladys Reece happy – as well, no doubt, as the Editor and the majority of readers of *The Dickensian* – by continuing to present Ellen's relationship with Dickens as pure and innocent. From Reece would have come the identification of the 'attached woman servant' whom Ley had earlier anonymously quoted, on her authority, as vouching on her deathbed for the fact that Ellen had never been Dickens's mistress. Her name, Morley now reveals, was Jane Wheeler, a native of Slough, who was to remain for many years, on and off, part of the Ternan household and who was especially devoted to Ellen. Morley could hardly ignore Aylmer's discovery of Dickens's frequent visits to Slough in the first half of 1867, but explains them as simply affording him 'snatched moments of rest, free from the noise and fanfare of fame'. As for 'Mr Tringham', Morley bluffly denies that there is any actual *proof* that Dickens ever used this name. It could, he writes, have been anyone – though why this anyone should be paying the Ternans' rates for them he does not explain.

Once he has got past Dickens's death, Morley can relax a bit and supply the first published account of the Ternans' subsequent history after Dickens's death. He can do so, of course, thanks to all the family records, photographs and personal recollections made available to him by Gladys Reece. So, for the first time, the new life that Ellen made for herself post 1870 becomes part of the record, though Morley seems unaware that she claimed to be much younger than she was. He relates her meeting, on a visit to her sister in Oxford, with an undergraduate called George Wharton Robinson, who was reading for holy orders, and her marriage to him in 1876, after she had persuaded him to resign from his curacy of St Anne's Church, Soho, and to become a schoolmaster instead. In his tenth and last article Morley writes about the period when Robinson was headmaster of a school in Margate, with Ellen responsible for teaching French and elocution. He cannot avoid the rock ahead of Canon Benham and his indiscreet talk with Thomas Wright, but tries to defuse the situation by focussing on Benham's celebrated fundraising Dickens readings and how he persuaded Ellen to join him in these entertainments. 'Her low attractive voice was combined with perfect diction' and she was soon much in demand for giving such performances, either with Benham or solo. He cannot avoid saying *something* about Thomas Wright's interview with Benham, but mentions it as neutrally as possible: Benham, he writes, 'also repeated some of the things related to him by Ellen about her friendship with Dickens'. And then he takes refuge in bluster:

Would an Anglican clergyman reveal to another person something that had been discussed with him, obviously in confidence, even though it had been years before? That 'confidence' went down the line, from Ellen to Benham, from Benham to Thomas Wright and from Wright to the world. How the news spreads. Slanderous whispers have been loudly shouted by gossips ever since. It is hearsay in the third degree and reiteration cannot make it any more than hearsay.

No doubt both Morley and Gladys Reece were much relieved that he could just ignore the other Gladys's book, *Dickens and Daughter*, since, unlike Georgina and Mamie, Kate Perugini did not apparently figure in Ellen's life after Dickens's death. This final instalment of Morley's chronicle describes the last years of all three Ternan sisters, especially the vicissitudes of the Robinsons' fortunes. Ellen and George had to leave Margate after George's health broke down and, after an attempt at running a day school in Maida Vale, they took up market gardening at Calcot, near Reading. Morley devotes much space to Gladys as a child prodigy, but mentions only *en passant* a number of fascinating details such as the fact that Ellen had close family on her father's side living in Rochester (it would later transpire that she was actually born there). Other details include the statement that Henry Dickens's children attended Ellen's Christmas parties, that Maria – remarkably, for a woman at this time – became a foreign correspondent for *The London Standard*, and that Ellen's son Geoffrey had a career in the army before he became first a bookseller and then a not very successful professional actor. After the death of his first wife, he became 'something of a recluse' but did marry again. His own death took place in 1959.

There could hardly be a bigger contrast in presentational qualities than between Morley's *Dickensian* series and the next important amateur contribution to the history of researches into the matter of Dickens and Ellen Ternan. This is an article with the title 'Dickens's Forgotten Retreat in France' which was written by William J. Carlton and published in the 1966 spring number of *The Dickensian*. Morley's articles are completely devoid of references, but Carlton's piece, like all his contributions to *The Dickensian* and other journals, is fully and meticulously documented. In 'Dickens's Forgotten Retreat in France' he writes about Dickens's relations with his genial Boulogne landlord M. Ferdinand Beaucourt-Mutuel. Dickens rented from him two different houses for successive family summer holidays between 1852 and 1856, and affectionately depicted him as M. Loyal Devasseur in his *Household Words* essay on Boulogne, 'Our French Watering Place' (4 November 1854). Carlton begins his article by drawing attention to what, on the face of it, would seem to be a prime example of that 'keeping up appearances' activity on the part of the Dickens family discussed in chapter 2 above.

We learn from him that in 1902 the editor of *Punch*, Sir Francis Burnand, a Dickens enthusiast, paid a holiday visit to the British owner of the Château d'Hardelot, located five or six miles south of Boulogne. Using the nom de plume of 'A Progressing Pilgrim', Burnand subsequently reported in the 17 September issue of *Punch*, in a column headed '"Boz" and Boulogne', that in the nearby village of Condette he had viewed the tombstone of Beaucourt-Mutuel who had died there in 1881 and whose memorial bears the following English inscription: 'The Landlord of whom Charles Dickens wrote, "I never did see such a kind gentle heart"'. Burnand followed this up in *Punch* for 1 October with a second '"Boz" and Boulogne' column relaying information he had since received that Beaucourt-Mutuel had owned 'a small country homestead' near Condette where Dickens had visited him and had liked the place so much that he stayed there for several days. Burnand had also learned that the Mayor of the commune of Condette, M. Huret-Laglache, 'a hale and hearty octogenarian', well remembered talking with Dickens in Beaucourt-Mutuel's rural retreat and that there were 'in the village of Hardelot . . . several persons possessing little souvenirs given to their parents by Charles Dickens'. Burnand then received a letter from M. Huret-Laglache himself confirming both that he had talked with Dickens in Condette and the existence of Dickens souvenirs among the local inhabitants. This was duly reported also in the 15 October issue of *Punch*.

In his column Burnand suggested that the Boz Club of which he was a member (it consisted mainly of men who had actually known Dickens and its committee was chaired by Sir Henry Dickens himself) might have an enjoyable outing to Condette, which idea, Carlton discovered, had been eagerly taken up by the Club's secretary Percy Fitzgerald and canvassed by him in some detail in the next issue of *The Boz Club Papers*. Nothing further was heard of the scheme, however, and Carlton surmises that it may have been vetoed by the Club's committee at the suggestion of Sir Henry who perhaps had his reasons for wishing to suppress all mention of Condette in connection with his father. Carlton shows that references to Dickens's visits to Condette and to the fact that the house where he had stayed was known locally (as it still is) as the 'Châlet Dickens' did appear in one or two places – in a 1903 letter to the London *Standard* and a 1905 history of the Château d'Hardelot – but it did not become part of the biographical record. Condette does not figure in the index to Johnson's *Charles Dickens*, for example.

Carlton goes on to draw attention to various letters written by Dickens between 1862 and 1865 and comments that, although 'characterised by an unwonted reticence and vagueness at such times as Dickens was proposing to absent himself from his accustomed haunts', they do provide 'irrefutable evidence that he made several visits to the continent during that period'. He proceeds to give several examples of Dickens telling correspondents that he has just returned from France or is just going there but without supplying much detail with regard to dates and places. He is going there 'on a little tour of observation' (to Sheridan Knowles, 7 July 1862) or he 'has been much in the country parts of France this summer' (to Hannah Brown, 24 October 1862). Carlton also notes that, writing to his more intimate friend Wilkie Collins on 20 September, Dickens makes a mysterious reference to 'some rather miserable anxieties' that he is suffering from and that he must tell Collins about at some point: 'I shall fight out of them, I daresay, being not easily beaten but they have gathered and gathered'. He was due to give a reading at the British Embassy in Paris on 17 January 1863 and told Thomas Beard on 24 December, 'I may be away a month or six weeks'. He wrote to Wilkie Collins on 1 January 1863 that on the following Sunday he would 'vanish into space for a day or two' before presenting himself in Paris on 15 January. On 6 January he wrote to his friend Sir Joseph Olliffe, physician to the British Embassy in Paris, that he was leaving home on Sunday 11 January 'to see a sick friend concerning whom I am anxious, and from whom I shall work my way round to Paris', which seems to indicate the 'sick friend' is in France. To another correspondent he writes on 9 January that he has 'made all kinds of pledges and promises to go to Lausanne a-visiting, afterwards [i.e., after the Embassy engagement], and perhaps to Geneva', but nothing more is ever heard of these.

Carlton continues to trace Dickens's wanderings with reference to his letters during this period; then, moving on to August, he notes that Dickens tells Collins on the 9th that, 'not having been anywhere for ever and ever so long', he is 'thinking of evaporating for a fortnight'. The next letters to which Carlton calls attention are some in late June 1864 telling one correspondent he is going to France 'for a few days' holiday' and another that he is 'just leaving here on a ten or twelve days' visit to Belgium'. Writing to Wills about the next Christmas Number of *All The Year Round*, the framing story of which was to feature again the London landlady Mrs Lirriper who had proved such a smash hit in the 1863 Number, Dickens suggests that the story might have a mingling in it of Paris and London. He adds, 'As my present Mysterious Disappearance is in that direction, I will turn this over on French ground with great care'. Carlton notes that Dickens also made 'short visits' to France in 1865 and cautiously notes that 'he may not always have been alone'. Clearly he was not so on that fateful Staplehurst day of 9 June.

Carlton does not explicitly connect all these 'vanishings into air' and 'Mysterious Disappearances' cited in the second section of his article with Condette or with Ellen, nor does he actually propose that Ellen was the 'sick friend' in France about whom Dickens was so anxious in January 1863, but his inferences are clear in the conclusion to his article. He points out there how little is known about Ellen's movements between 1857 and 1870, also that 'the disclosures made by Thomas Wright, Gladys Storey, Professor Ada Nisbet, Sir Felix Aylmer and others concerning the association between Dickens and Ellen Ternan relate almost entirely to the period following the Staplehurst accident'. As far as his own research is concerned, Carlton writes, 'the studied vagueness of some of Dickens's references to his cross-channel expeditions and the enigmatic phrasing of others must inevitably give rise to the suspicion that he had something to hide, especially when it is remembered that from 1860 onwards he systematically destroyed all letters and papers received by him'.

Carlton's reference to the reports and findings of Wright and Storey as 'acutely controversial' was no doubt meant as a sop to those diehard Dickensians who were still committed to the idea that the association between Dickens and Ellen was entirely innocent, but if so, it did not work. He was taken to task in the next issue of *The Dickensian* by a regular contributor to the journal called Frank A. Gibson, who maintained that in his relations with Ellen, Dickens, being worldly-wise, simply 'wished to shield the young woman whom he had befriended and whom he loved'. He did shield her and, Gibson gallantly adds, 'all the more intelligent Dickensians since then have refrained from writing her name unnecessarily'. Gibson's was already a lost cause by this time, however, and there have been plenty of references to Ellen in *The Dickensian* during the last fifty years or so. As to the 'Châlet Dickens', it had become generally accepted by students of Dickens's life by the time Fred Kaplan published his *Dickens: A Biography* in 1988 that Dickens had used it as a hideaway for himself and Ellen during the early 1860s (see Kaplan's *Dickens*, chapter 13) and it was billed as 'the love-nest' during a recent academic Dickens conference in Boulogne. No actual evidence has ever emerged, however, that Ellen ever set foot in the place, and the only hint that she might have done so remains that mysteriously abrupt abandonment by the Boz Club in 1902 of the projected outing to Condette which was the starting-point for Carlton's detailed investigations.

The discoveries made by Felix Aylmer, coming on top of those of Ada Nisbet, and the conclusion drawn by both of them – namely that this new material proved Dickens and Ellen to have been lovers – caused Edward Wagenknecht, Professor of English at Boston University and author of *The Man Charles Dickens* (see above, p. 110), to publish a revised version of his essay 'Dickens and the Scandalmongers', originally printed in the April 1950 issue of *College English*. In it Wagenknecht had robustly attacked various Dickens biographers, including Pope-Hennessy, for accepting as true those statements about Dickens and Ellen which Wright and Storey respectively reported Canon Benham and Kate Perugini as having made. He had asserted that his primary concern was 'the responsible use of evidence in criticism and biography' and insisted that 'the only possible verdict' with regard to the question of whether Dickens and

Ellen were lovers was '*not proven*'. In 1965 he published a revised version of this essay as the lead article in his *Dickens and the Scandalmongers: Essays in Criticism* (1965). Nisbet's evidence, he argued, showed that 'in some sense of the term, Dickens "loved" Ellen Ternan' but it certainly did not 'prove they had sexual relations', any more than did Aylmer's discoveries about Dickens renting a cottage in Slough under the name of Tringham. Wagenknecht reiterated that he was primarily concerned with 'the integrity of scholarship', but his combative stance certainly laid him open to George H. Ford's amusing comparison of him (in a review of *Dickens and the Scandalmongers* in *Nineteenth Century Fiction*) to Othello demanding that Iago should give him 'ocular proof' of Desdemona's infidelity. 'Lovers', Ford sagely observes, '(and Victorian lovers in particular) do not ordinarily provide the kind of evidence Wagenknecht expects his opponents to come up with'.

CHAPTER EIGHT

What Gladys knew:
The Storey Papers

Despite all the facts unearthed by Morley about her early stage career and her post-Dickens years as a happy wife and mother, Ellen herself remained a somewhat shadowy figure. On 7 February 1957, however, readers of *The Evening News* did get a glimpse of her as a person in her own right in an article contributed by a literary-minded barrister named C. G. L. Du Cann to a series the paper was running called 'The World's Strangest Stories'. His piece was headed 'Was Dickens a Wicked Man?' in allusion to Kate Perugini's remark, reported by Storey, 'My father was a wicked man'. It was illustrated by a picture of Ellen captioned 'Ellen Ternan . . . no proof of scandal'. Posing the question as to 'what sort of person' Ellen had been, Du Cann wrote:

> I have recently spoken with Ellen Ternan's own daughter and with another lady who lived with Ellen.
>
> They say that she was gentle, good and sweet. She was swift and clever in talk; interested in books; and had a definite will of her own.

She cared little about money and was not, as some biographers have suggested, in the least like Dickens characters
Bella Wilfer, Estella Provis or Helena Landless (in spite of the
similarity of the last name).

In the last sentence he is alluding to Ellen's middle name
'Lawless'. In his subsequent book, *The Love Lives of Charles
Dickens*, published by Storey's publisher Frederick Muller in
1961, Du Cann states that, although he had been initially
convinced by Lord Jowitt's 1953 judgment in *The Sunday Times*
that Ellen had been Dickens's mistress, he now no longer
believed this to have been the case. He had interviewed Storey
and had concluded that she had simply accepted Kate's story
'without question'. As she had failed to cross-examine Kate on
the source of her alleged knowledge of Dickens's relationship
with Ellen, 'it could only be hearsay at most'. Du Cann then
invokes his conversations with Ellen's daughter in order to evoke
an image of Ellen very different from the 'greedy, gold-digging,
frivolous creature' of the scandalmongers:

Throughout life she [Ellen] was a strong-minded intellectual,
even puritanical, woman fully conscious of her own value, and
easily dominating her husband and other males of her acquaintance. She was well able to withstand any man's will-power,
having plenty of her own. She was not in the least mercenary,
as the biographers have falsely assumed from Dickens' later
young heroines [in fact, it is only Bella Wilfer in *Our Mutual
Friend* who is – initially and not very seriously – mercenary].
Indeed she was quite the contrary.

Ellen's actual character and personality is then vividly evoked by
Du Cann's printing of a warmly affectionate, newsy letter
written by her on 26 June 1913 to her 'own darlingest Geoffrey'

when he was serving as a Sandhurst-trained Army officer in Ireland. At this time Ellen, having been widowed six years earlier, was living in modest retirement in Southsea together with Fanny, who was also widowed and now ailing (Maria had died in 1904). Some French ships were making a courtesy visit to Portsmouth at the time and Ellen tells her son how she had gaily greeted some French sailors in the street with the words, 'Vive la France, vive la Marine Française et vive M. Poincaré', and how charmingly they had responded. She also recommends Geoffrey to read a new Kipling poem in *The Morning Post*, gives news of his Aunt Fanny and relays loving messages from her, encloses a picture cut out from an illustrated paper that she thinks he'll enjoy, and ends the letter 'With all my heart's love, / Always your loving/ Mother'.

Du Cann does not say where he saw this letter but was presumably shown it by the widow of Geoffrey's second marriage. He mentions Geoffrey's chequered post-Army career, first as a bookseller and then as an actor under the stage-name of 'Terence Cliborne' [Du Cann's error for 'Clibburn']. He must have got this information partly from Geoffrey's widow and partly from Gladys Reece, and perhaps also from Malcolm Morley, who was a friend of his. He also learned that Geoffrey had suffered from chronic ill-health as well as financial difficulties, and that he had been utterly appalled and horrified by the upsurge of scandal about Dickens and his mother in the mid-1930s. He categorically refused to discuss it, according to Du Cann, even with his wife or his sister, and preserved 'an iron and religious silence' on the subject until he died. Evidently, Storey had chosen not to enlighten Du Cann as to why Geoffrey should have behaved like this. With her knowledge of Geoffrey's momentous interview with Sir Henry, she certainly could have done so but instead left him undisturbed in his lofty conviction that the reason for Geoffrey's silence was that 'a gentleman does not dispute over his mother's honour'.

The survival of that one lovely warm letter from his mother may be the result of accident or it may be that Geoffrey just could not bring himself to destroy it. A few years after its publication by Du Cann some rather different letters of Ellen's came to light. In 1965 Leshie C. Staples published in *The Dickensian* a somewhat odd correspondence that she had conducted in November and December 1872 with George Smith, a leading London publisher. As Staples notes, this exchange of letters does 'present a picture, however slight' of Ellen's personality. In the end, however, it raises rather more questions than it answers about what she was really like and also about how, where and with whom she lived during the years between Dickens's death when she was, in fact, thirty-one though giving her age as twenty-one, and her marriage five and a half years later to twenty-five-year-old George Wharton Robinson. Why, in the first place, was she asking Smith if he would anonymously publish a poem written by an unnamed friend of hers when the friend in question was the well-established poet Alfred Austin, later to become Poet Laureate (a preposterously unworthy successor to Tennyson)? Smith accepted the poem for publication on the conditions proposed whereupon Ellen promptly revealed Austin's identity. Smith at once withdrew his acceptance of the poem, clearly irritated – with some justification, one feels – by having been subjected to what he evidently considered a time-wasting trick. Ellen, on her side, seems to have felt a sense of injured merit and proceeded to embroil the publisher in further correspondence in which, with notable eloquence, she defended herself against what she considered to be the injustice of his implied reproach.

The next discovery relating directly to the Dickens scandal did not add much to our scanty knowledge of Ellen's character and personality, though it was certainly notable for other reasons. It came about in a rather remarkable way. After Gladys Storey died in November 1978 her heir, the well-known publisher Charles Monteith, hired David Hunt, a contractor, to move some furniture from her St John's Wood home. In one of the pieces to be moved Mr Hunt discovered a cache of papers and old notebooks and was asked to dispose of this material as waste paper. Noticing that the name of Dickens occurred frequently in some of the papers and remembering his wife's interest in this subject, Mr Hunt decided to take this archive home. Having looked through it, Mrs Hunt thought it might be of significance to scholars and took it to the Dickens Museum in Doughty Street where the Curator, Dr David Parker, soon confirmed that it was indeed of considerable interest. Subsequently the Hunts, acting jointly with Mr Monteith, generously donated the archive to the Museum and a general description of its contents co-authored by Dr Parker and myself appeared in the Spring 1980 issue of *The Dickensian*.

Four fragile sheets of notes in Storey's hand collected in a green loose-leaf binder contain the raw material, as it were, for the passages relating to Ellen that were subsequently published in *Dickens and Daughter*. At the head of these notes Storey writes, 'Related by K.P. to my mother and me at 9.30 Sunday evening Feb 18th 1923. Re. C.D.'s life – A Revelation – and unknown to the World.' The notes themselves show that Kate Perugini did not actually name Ellen in this first burst of confidence but referred to her only as 'a young girl' whom Dickens 'took up with'. A later note added by Storey reads, 'C.D. kept an establishment one with two servants for her at Peckham'. Not all the Ellen-related material in these notes appears in *Dickens and Daughter*, however. One such passage, not quoted in the *Dickensian* account of the archive, is rather poignant: 'When Mrs C.D. left for good C.D. she never saw him again but once at the theatre with Ellen Ternan when Mrs C.D. was so overcome that she was obliged to leave the theatre'. Another such passage confirmed that Ellen did indeed come to Gad's Hill when Dickens was dying, but she certainly did not do so under Kate's escort as Pope-Hennessy had described her as doing:

> C.D. kept up with the other woman until his death & settled money on her. When he was dying K.P. & her sister went to him in the dining room at Gad's H where he lay on a sofa – they cut his coat and a letter from K.P. was the only one found in his pocket. Directly he was dead K.P. went to her mother & during that time the other woman came to see him – she would not have come had I been there said K.P.

Storey's notes continue on from this passage without a break, though Kate's comments are now evidently connected with an earlier period: 'Later on after the separation C.D. was miserable – a miserable man'. The extent of her distress and remorse over the way her mother was treated at the time of the separation can be seen from the extreme-sounding nature of some of her statements here recorded by Storey: 'Except [for] the childhood of M[amie] and K.P. the home life of C.D. could not be surpassed in the unhappiness of everyday life'.

In Storey's notes this statement comes just before the following passage quoted only in part in the above-mentioned *Dickensian* article, and containing a startling and very important piece of information that, as we have seen, she had confided to Walter Dexter in 1939 but that had not yet been made public:

> K.P. is in constant dread of the truth coming to light & of his reputation falling from his pedestal – the other woman married – & is now dead the son came to H.F.D. [i.e. Henry Fielding Dickens] the only surviving son of C.D. & asked if it was true that his mother was the mistress of C.D. & H.F.D. had to admit it – But KP says – that when the time comes – the truth *must* be told.

At this point Storey later added an additional, only half-punctuated, marginal note, here quoted from the manuscript which differs slightly from the transcription given in *The Dickensian*:

Henry F. Dickens told me this at 8 Mulberry Walk [his home] on Sunday Sept 8 [Storey's error for Sept 9] 1928 told me he replied "Unfortunately yes" Geoffrey E.T.'s son asked Sir Henry "Was my mother your father's mistress Sir Henry replied (he told me) I had to say "Unfortunately yes".

On a separate sheet of paper inserted into this green binder there are some notes, originally written in pencil and then inked over, that appear to be the original ones made by Storey immediately following her remarkable conversation with a clearly very stressed Sir Henry on the evening of Sunday 9 September 1928, just after the publication on the preceding Friday of *This Side Idolatry* and Sir Henry's outraged response in the Saturday edition of *The Daily News* (see above, p. 60). Storey's account of her Sunday evening visit to Sir Henry is summarised in the 1980 *Dickensian* article, but full quotation is needed to bring out the drama of the scene:

Lady Dickens rang up and said they wanted to see me on the way to Kitty's (Mrs P's) & mother, too – so we went to 8, Mulberry Walk. Lady D. – with her foot up. Sir Henry came forward with notes in his left hand & shook hands with the right. He commenced right away on the attack on his father by Mr B. Roberts in his book 'This side Idolatry'. He said 'I am worried to death' & started to read what he had written in answer to Mr Roberts's 'Challenge' to him. He [i.e., Roberts] asked him to let him see the letters from 'either my father or my mother ['] \ he added that he would not know his mother's handwriting/ a reporter from the 'Daily News' who had sent

Sir Henry a copy of the book \ called & / sent in his card to ask whether he was going to let the press have his answer to 'Ephesian' he [i.e., Sir Henry] said he would not see him but had not noticed his message on the back \ of the card / so he replied to return later for an answer. Lady D went out \ to him/ & said probably tomorrow – so he [i.e., the *Daily News* reporter] said it was as well as the Sunday papers would not get it. Sir Henry and I (mother left to go to Mrs P's) talked about Ellen Ternan – that there was a boy but it died – & she married a man called Robinson – Geoffrey Robinson asked Sir H 'was my mother your father's mistress [?'] & said Sir Henry I had to say in reply 'Unfortunately yes ['']. Sir Henry told me G.S. while Lady D was getting ready – pouring with rain.

A variant version of this conversation that seems to indicate that Lady Dickens was, in fact, present throughout appears in a notebook into which Storey seems to have copied material from elsewhere:

Sir Henry then spoke about Ellen Ternan the girl Dickens really lived with – Sir H. said there was a boy (as Mrs P. had told me) but he died and Ellen Ternan married a man called Robinson – Lady D. told me that Georgina Hogarth introduced Lady D to Ellen Ternan when she was Mrs Robinson and that Geoffrey the son of Mrs R called on Sir H after her death & this son met Sir Henry's children on the sands once! Then Sir Henry spoke of Georgina Hogarth – who was supposed to have a son by C.D. . . . who turned up not many years back – but he said I have written something to be brought forward after my death to refute it.

This document of Sir Henry's writing has yet to come to light, but must have been the one he had drawn up in 1908 for transmission to Calcutta at the time of the Charley Peters fraud, perhaps accompanied by a certificate of virginity for Georgina (see above, p. 99).

As we have seen in chapter 3, Sir Henry took refuge, in the Monday edition of *The Daily News*, in simply dismissing Bechhofer Roberts's book as 'utterly unworthy of the slightest consideration'. More significantly for the history of the scandal, there is no mention in *Dickens and Daughter* that he, too, had told Storey that Ellen had had a child by Dickens and that the child had died. As regards this information, it would have been difficult for Storey to publish it with Geoffrey Robinson still very much alive, however uncommunicative. Yet if she had said in *Dickens and Daughter* that she had been told not only by Kate but *also* by Sir Henry that Ellen had borne Dickens a child that had died in infancy, it would surely have given pause to those who hastened to dismiss her as having distorted the ramblings of a distressed and possibly confused old lady. Probably, she refrained from quoting Sir Henry out of consideration for the feelings of his widow who, in a letter to Storey quoted in the 1980 *Dickensian* article, had strongly deplored all raking over the details of Dickens's personal life:

> As for the silly Beadnell love affair & the Ternan affair everyone has heard these stories over & over again, 4 generations know about it published in letters, in books & in papers, & now you give it to a 5th generation! Every one of these people are no more. Why not speak only of Charles Dickens for the good he did to the poor, & the sufferers; his books belong *to all* but his private life to himself *alone*. . . .

Storey no doubt defended herself to Lady Dickens on the grounds of the solemn promise or pledge she had made to Kate

Perugini to tell the world the truth at last about Dickens and his beloved Ellen.

For those who today take an interest in this matter, Sir Henry's testimony as reported by Storey, writing almost 'to the minute' like a latter-day Samuel Richardson heroine, must strengthen the case for believing Kate's words as recorded in *Dickens and Daughter*. Nor was this the only new evidence in the Storey Papers for a short-lived love-child having been born to Dickens and Ellen. Also present are copies of two letters to Walter Dexter from a certain C. E. S. Chambers, the first of which is dated 21 January 1934. Chambers was writing in response to an article by Dexter in *The Daily Mail* denying that any 'other woman' had been involved in the collapse of the Dickens marriage. He was a great-nephew of Janet, wife of W. H. Wills, and a cousin of Rudolph Lehmann. He and Lehmann had acquired the whole archive of Dickens's letters to Wills which, as mentioned above, Lehmann then edited for publication in 1912. Chambers told Dexter that 'certain members of my family had great intimacy with C.D. and remember being told many years ago by an old aunt (Mrs Fred Lehmann of 15 Berkeley Square) that C.D. had actually lived for some 12 years with a well-known actress, I forget the name'. 'Mrs Fred Lehmann' was Nina Lehmann, née Chambers, mother of Rudolph and niece of Janet Wills. She and her husband Frederick became good friends of Dickens's daughters and members of the Dickens circle generally.

Chambers goes on to tell Dexter that he and Lehmann had discovered some of Dickens's letters to Wills to be 'of an extremely private nature' in that they contained instructions to Wills written from America during Dickens's 1867/8 visit 'regarding the welfare of a certain lady, then apparently sickening for her confinement'. The instructions were 'of the most intimate nature', and Chambers and Lehmann thought the half-dozen letters involved should not have been preserved. Their best course, they decided, would be to send them to Sir Henry Dickens and, wrote Chambers, 'that we did, and what became of them only his [Sir Henry's] executors can now tell!' Dexter's response has not survived, but he evidently asked if the name of the lady concerned was Ellen or Ellen Ternan and whether it was she who had been the cause of Dickens's separation from his wife. Chambers replied that the separation was 'from incompatibility and nothing else'. He wrote that according to the gossip in the Chambers family, which was evidently a little wild, Catherine was 'wholly illiterate' and Dickens 'used to say, that looking round his dinner table at a row of vacant faces wanting in intelligence made his heart sick!' He scouted the idea that Dickens would have had any 'intimacy' either before or after the separation with Georgina, whom he remembered only as 'a horribly ugly old woman'. As to the lady who was 'sickening for her confinement' in the winter of 1867/8, he could not remember her name but wrote, 'I . . . fancy somehow it was the same as mentioned in your letter, no doubt she is long dead'.

Other documents in this Storey archive relate to the writing and publication of *Dickens and Daughter* and include correspondence between Storey and her publisher Frederick Muller, who had clearly become anxious about some legal aspects of the book. This anxiety increased after his usual printers had withdrawn from the job because they were nervous about it. Storey resisted Muller's urging of her to write a preface, but she did agree to a clause in the contract indemnifying him against any action brought for obscenity or libel, though she thought this unnecessary. 'The part of the book referring to Ellen Ternan and Dickens is most obscene and indecent!' she wrote, adding, 'But in any case *nobody can sue anybody in respect of a libel upon a person who is dead.*' She was, of course, quite correct in this. But she nevertheless showed restraint in not quoting some of the things

Kate had said about Georgina Hogarth, who was, according to Kate, 'without doubt in love with C.D.'. This would seem to be confirmed by a letter Storey received from Thackeray's granddaughter Hester Fuller (quoted in the 1980 *Dickensian* article) congratulating her on the publication of *Dickens and Daughter*:

How *wicked* it was of Miss Hogarth not to withdraw – but my mother said she was in love with C.D. & was always charming & well & beautifully dressed, while Mrs C.D. was a weak and overwhelmed woman never out of having a child.

Georgina's sad end – she lived to be ninety and, so Kate told Storey on 8 July 1928, 'went slightly cookoo [*sic*] at the end' – evidently haunted Kate. She dreaded losing her mind as Georgina had done because she (Georgina) would sometimes 'rave about C.D.' and Kate feared that if she met a similar fate, she herself might blurt out indiscretions about her father. A marginal note added by Storey to the notes in the green binder details one of the more sensational of poor Georgina's 'ravings': 'Coming out of a stupor Georgina said "My child, my child. Tell me, is it a boy or a girl." K.P. said she did not know where [she] could have had it.'

Among the letters in the Storey Papers are some relating to her interview with Dexter at the Dickens House before the book's publication (see chapter 5 above) during which, she told Hester Fuller, she asked him what he would say about it in *The Dickensian* and he answered, 'The truth at last'. To her disappointment, she wrote, not only did he *not* say this in the journal but he published in it a carping and critical review by Ley. Copies of letters from Storey to George Bernard Shaw are also present in this archive enlisting his help in defending her against criticisms of her book in *The Times Literary Supplement*, as well as letters indicating that she was intending to bring out a second edition of *Dickens and*

Daughter, there being, as she wrote to Ada Nisbet in January 1960, 'more Truth to tell'. She also transcribes a note from Shaw apparently sent to the Manuscript Department of the British Museum in 1963: 'Glad to hear that a new edition of D & D is coming out & proud to figure in it'. To this Storey appends a brief sentence: 'I am at work upon it.' There is little evidence, however, of such work in these papers (by this time she was quite elderly and not in good health) and none at all that in a new edition she would have been able to substantiate Kate Perugini's reported claim that Dickens and Ellen had a son who died in infancy – apart, that is, from her notes of what Sir Henry had told her. The only reply she vouchsafed to W. H. Bowen in 1950, when he was researching the medical histories of Dickens and his relatives and had written to ask her what evidence she had to support Kate's bald statement that Ellen had borne Dickens a son, was a grandly vague assertion: 'All is based on truth.'

The account of the Storey Papers in the Spring 1980 number of *The Dickensian* was immediately followed in that issue by a letter to the editor from Katharine M. Longley, writing from the Borthwick Institute of Historical Research in York, who announced that she had for thirteen years 'been researching the friendship of Dickens with the Ternan family'. She had also examined the Storey Papers at the Dickens House and was anxious to comment on some of them 'before a fresh wave of scandal breaks over the names of Ellen Ternan and Charles Dickens'. She was referring specifically to the Chambers letters to Dexter showing that Dickens had been concerned about a lady 'sickening for her confinement' while he was in America during the winter of 1867/8. Drawing on information she had found in a series of unpublished letters written by Fanny Trollope to her step-daughter Beatrice ('Bice'), Longley showed that Ellen and her mother had gone to stay with Fanny in Florence in late October or early November 1867 and remained there until

24 April 1868. She omits to mention the fact that Ada Nisbet had already demonstrated, through her decipherment of the instructions to Wills in Dickens's 1867 diary, that Ellen was in Florence staying with her sister Fanny and her brother-in-law at the Villa Trollope. By reference to some unpublished letters of Fanny's that she has seen, however, Longley is able to show that Ellen was certainly not living a secluded life at the Villa Trollope but on the contrary participating very fully in the life of the Anglo-Florentine society of the day. Very much at the centre of this life was Browning's great friend the society hostess Isa Blagden, whose letters show her to have been a great gossip. A couple of years later, for example, she enjoyed enlightening Browning as to why Fanny had got such good rates from Dickens for her fiction in *All The Year Round* – it was, she wrote, because Fanny was Ellen's sister, a relationship of which Browning confessed he had been completely unaware. Longley comments:

> Had Ellen Ternan produced an illegitimate baby while in Florence under Isa's observation, there would never have been a Ternan 'mystery'; a public scandal commensurate with the fame of Charles Dickens would have been the immediate result.

Longley then addresses the question as to why Sir Henry might have believed that the pregnancy referred to in those letters to Wills sent to him by Chambers and Lehmann related to Ellen and would therefore have destroyed them. Her argument is that there is no evidence that until he saw these letters Sir Henry, who was only nine years old when his parents separated, believed that Ellen and his father were lovers. There is, however, some circumstantial evidence to the contrary: 'He cannot possibly have believed this in the days when he permitted his younger daughters to attend the Christmas parties given by

Ellen, as Mrs Wharton Robinson, for her own little daughter Gladys (born in 1884)'. Longley believes, in other words, that in 1911/12 when he was sent the letters, Sir Henry must just have jumped to the startling conclusion that the lady in question was Ellen. Since, given where she was during the winter of 1867/8, we know this simply could not have been the case, Longley proposes that the expectant mother in question must have been Dickens's daughter-in-law Bessie, Charley's wife, whose fifth child, Gertrude Dorothy Maria, was born on 7 February 1868. As to the baby boy who died, about whom Sir Henry also spoke to Storey but who is not mentioned by Chambers in his letters to Dexter, Longley argues that Sir Henry might also have found a reference to such an ill-fated infant in the letters sent to him and got it mixed up with the references to the expectant mother (sheets from different letters perhaps getting jumbled up together). The baby in question might well have been Richard Spofford Spofford, the only child of Ellen's cousin Richard Smith Spofford, who died on 10 September 1867 aged only eight months, and this sad event might have been canvassed by Dickens in his correspondence with Wills as a possible pretext for Ellen's coming to America.

No matter how much or how little we may find ourselves persuaded by Longley's arguments here (other than by the completely convincing one about the impossibility of Ellen's having had a baby in Florence under the eyes of Isa Blagden during the winter of 1867/8), we can see in this intervention of hers the emergence of a formidably well-briefed (and evidently strongly-motivated) champion of the purity of Ellen's relationship with Dickens. And as the next chapter will show, she was able, in advancing her case, to draw on a mass of hitherto unpublished and highly pertinent primary material to which she alone had access.

CHAPTER NINE

Nelly visible

Like Aylmer, Katharine Longley was a great aficionado of detective stories and enjoyed referring to her 'Marplish' streak. Like Aylmer again, her first forays into matters Dickensian had been concerned with solving the puzzle posed by the unfinished *Mystery of Edwin Drood*. This led her on to becoming interested in that other great mystery of Dickens's later years, the nature and history of his relationship with Ellen. As an archivist by profession, she had the research skills needed for investigating the subject and acquired another great advantage when she made the acquaintance of an elderly lady named Helen Wickham. Helen's mother had become a bosom friend of Ellen's very shortly after Dickens's death. Helen herself had been born in 1884, the same year as Ellen's daughter Gladys, and the two girls had been life-long devoted friends. She often stayed with the Robinsons, sometimes on quite long visits. Later, she shared Gladys's distress at the way in which Ellen was depicted by Wright and succeeding Dickens biographers. She remonstrated about this with the prolific biographer (and close friend of Hugh Kingsmill) Hesketh Pearson following the publication of his *Charles Dickens: His*

Character, Comedy, and Career in 1949 in which he wrote: 'Apparently, Ellen placed comfort before chastity. This is evident from the fact of her surrender . . . .' His response to Helen's objection was simply to refer her to Wright's book. In 1961 Gladys did find a defender of her mother's honour in the barrister-author Charles Du Cann, as mentioned in the last chapter, but his book seems to have made little impact. Now Longley, after becoming acquainted with Helen in 1968, took up the matter with tenacious enthusiasm. Helen was happy to confide to her safe-keeping – and, eventually, to give her outright – the Robinson family archive that she herself had inherited from Gladys after the latter's death in 1973. This archive Longley donated, together with her own Ternan archive, to what is now the Senate House Library of the University of London. It includes an extensive collection of Ternan and Robinson family photographs as well as Ellen's commonplace books for 1871–73 and George Wharton Robinson's for 1870–74, also Ellen's address book for 1910–13 and Gladys's diaries for 1907–10. All this material, we notice, apart from some of the family photographs, relates to Ellen's life *after* Dickens's death, but nevertheless it helps enormously to bring her into focus as a person in her own right.

By 1980 Longley had completed work on a revised version of an exhaustively researched and massively documented manuscript, approximately 300,000 words long, which she eventually entitled *A Pardoner's Tale: Charles Dickens and the Ternan Family*. Her 'Foreword' explains the Chaucerian echo in her title while at the same time indicating what must inevitably be a fatal flaw in any research programme, namely the existence in the researcher's mind of a foregone conclusion. Longley had been moved by Helen Wickham's glowing memories of Ellen as a much-loved honorary aunt and announces that she is writing as Ellen's 'defence counsel' as regards the relationship with Dickens. She is, in other words, setting out to prove a negative, a notoriously difficult enterprise but one which she tackles with indefatigable enthusiasm. She was under no illusion, either, that the result would be anywhere near as attractive to publishers as would have been the case if she had written a book containing evidence supporting the idea that Dickens and Ellen *had* been lovers. 'What I have proved', she wrote ruefully to Madeline House, one of the editors of the Pilgrim Edition of Dickens's letters, on 30 June 1974, 'is that CD compromised ET. A permissive age just won't be interested in this . . . .' Moreover, the sheer length of her work, half of it consisting of footnotes and appendices, made it virtually unpublishable, even by a university press, and she eventually turned to *The Dickensian* as an outlet for her findings.

As noted in the previous chapter, Longley's 'Letter to the Editor' in the journal's Spring 1980 issue effectively disposed of the notion that Ellen might have had a baby while Dickens was away in America during the winter of 1867–68. Another 'Letter to the Editor' a year later announced an important discovery, namely that Dickens, besides renting Elizabeth Cottage for himself in Slough during 1866–67, had also, as evidenced by local rate-books, been involved in the renting by Ellen and her mother of another cottage in the same little town during the very same period. This second cottage stood in Church Street about a quarter of a mile away from Elizabeth Cottage, and Longley notes the strange coincidence that it was in Church Street, Slough, many years later, that Ellen's son Geoffrey would make his attempt at running a bookshop. She had discovered that from about February 1866 the rates on the Church Street cottage were paid by 'Tringham', the same alias Dickens was using to pay the Elizabeth Cottage rates, and then, from about May 1866 onwards, they were paid by 'Turnan'.

Longley does not speculate about motivation in her 'Letter to the Editor', but it seems likely that Ellen and her mother would have moved to Slough for reasons of economy (and also, no doubt, to be close to Dickens's bolt-hole) after Mrs Ternan had finished her engagement at the Lyceum Theatre – and had, in fact, retired from the stage altogether – at the end of 1865. Ellen's house in Houghton Place could meanwhile be made a source of income through being let to tenants. In the series of unpublished letters from Fanny Trollope to her step-daughter already mentioned (above, p. 160) Longley notes one in which Fanny tells Beatrice that she was staying in Slough with 'Mamma and Ellen' in late May and early June 1867. The Church Street cottage was, Longley notes, 'clearly the family home at this time' and it would, of course, have been fine for Dickens to visit the Ternans there, quite respectably, whenever he was in Slough. As regards the 'Tringham' alias, Longley also published in the 1981 *Dickensian* a short article suggesting that Dickens got this from the name of a tobacconist who in the early 1860s kept a shop near to the office of his weekly journal *All The Year Round*. The name, Longley believes, would have resonated with Dickens at this time, when he might have been apprehensive about possible scandalmongering in Slough, because it was the name given by Thomas Hood to a 'prattling, tattling village' in his poem 'A Tale of a Trumpet' which would certainly have been known to Dickens, a great friend and admirer of Hood's.

Helen Wickham died in 1982 and three years later Longley published in *The Dickensian* a long, densely footnoted article, 'The Real Ellen Ternan'. Her title was intended to imply that the image of Ellen prevalent in Dickens biographies was a false one. In this, the first real attempt to depict Ellen as a person in her own right rather than as a connection of Dickens's, Longley drew on her many years of correspondence and conversations with Helen Wickham to present a most attractive figure, a lively and charming woman with a great sense of fun which she evidently enjoyed expressing in light verse, or even downright doggerel. She was intelligent and apparently very well read in both English and French literature. She emerges as a loving but not uncritical wife ('George is so *silly*', she once remarked), a devoted mother and friend, and someone who, in spite of her delicate health (perhaps, Longley speculates, resulting from injuries sustained in the Staplehurst accident), was for many years a highly popular and accomplished giver of public readings from Dickens, among other writers, in aid of various local charities. *The Thanet Free Press* had hailed her on 5 December 1885 as someone 'ever ready to assist in all good works'.

Longley quotes Helen Wickham as fondly remembering Ellen as 'one of the most warm-hearted and generous women I have ever known, ready to empty her purse for those in need', also as someone who had 'such wit, fire and intense vitality'. Her memories of Ellen were not all rose-coloured, however. She had apparently a tendency to domineer over her household and to let George 'make a perfect doormat of himself for her'. She was also capable of making 'extraordinary scenes' when she could not get her own way. Helen Wickham told Longley that the physical description of Lucie Manette in *A Tale of Two Cities*, especially with regard to a certain characteristic facial expression described by Dickens, was an exact physical portrait of Ellen (baffled seekers after the 'real' Ellen have often lamented that in all other respects Lucie is among the most null of Dickens's heroines). Ellen had apparently been very deprecatory about her own appearance when young. Her sister Maria had been 'handsome', she had once said, and Fanny had been '*lovely*' but she herself had had no claim to prettiness, having had 'the figure of an oak tree and a complexion like a copper saucepan'. When she became pregnant in 1878 there had been worries about her delicate health, but she herself had been overjoyed, saying that she would 'love to have a whole nursery-full of children' – a remark that has considerable poignancy, of course, if one believes that in another, earlier, existence she had had to suffer the loss of an illegitimate child.

Devoted wife and mother though she was, Ellen Robinson was apparently 'not at all a domesticated person', according to Helen Wickham. Very unlike a Dickensian heroine, she was happy to leave most household arrangements to servants, notably the faithful Jane Brown, née Wheeler, who had first worked for her and her mother in Slough. What she liked best was lively chat with her sisters and other visitors about 'topics of the day, politics, literature and the arts, especially music and drama', or else playing parlour games, often of a quite demanding nature intellectually. Longley notes that Ellen's commonplace book with its anthology of quotations from eminent British and French writers gives evidence of wide and serious reading in both languages (we might recall here that Kate Perugini is reported by Storey to have once said that Ellen had brains which she had used to educate herself). English writers cited in the commonplace book include Huxley, Hume, Carlyle, Arnold, Froude, Macaulay, Shakespeare, Tennyson, Shelley and Wordsworth, while among the French are George Sand, Hugo, Rousseau, Beaumarchais and Michelet. After Dickens's death Ellen seems to have spent much time in Oxford visiting Maria, and many of her comic verse compositions relate to Oxford student life, notably to rowing, which was George Robinson's favourite activity at the time. Newspaper clippings pasted into the book show that some of her verses were published in the local press. One little poem Longley notes as being of particular interest to Dickensians in that it is an elegy, written on mourning paper, for Mamie Dickens's cherished little Pomeranian dog, Mrs Bouncer:

> We miss your soft and dainty step,
>   Your bright eye's loving gaze,
> Your pretty head, your graceful mien,
>   Your thousand winning ways . . .

Longley notes that Ellen's address book for 1910–13 and her birthday book, which Longley had on microfilm, both show that she kept in touch not only with Georgina and Mamie but also with many other members of the Dickens family, including Sir Henry and all his family and even Harriet, the blind wife whom Dickens's youngest brother Augustus had deserted when he ran off to Chicago with another woman in 1858. Kate Perugini's name, however, is notably absent from the book.

Yet when sixteen-year-old Helen Wickham went to stay with the Robinsons in 1900 she was warned by her mother, 'You must not bother Aunt Ellen about Dickens. She doesn't wish to remember those days – it makes her so sad'. Instead of the 'great treat' that she was anticipating of hearing Ellen read aloud from Dickens, Helen found herself having to listen, along with Gladys, to a reading of one of Fanny Trollope's novels called *The Wild Wheel* published in 1892. It was, Longley notes, 'a remarkable choice . . . for its plot hinges entirely on the effect upon a respectable family of the seduction of one of its members by a married man, and his attempt to make some amends towards them by a legacy, which they repudiate'. In her *Pardoner's Tale*, from which this *Dickensian* article is, of course, quarried, Longley comments: 'If the Ellen who chose to read the book aloud to her sixteen-year-old daughter and her friend had ever herself been seduced by a married man (who made her a well-known bequest) her mind must have been not so much complex as warped'. In her *Dickensian* article she relates that Helen Wickham had once told her that the nearest she had ever come to hearing 'Aunt Ellen' say anything about Dickens was when she discovered a photograph of him and his daughters at Gad's Hill. Upon seeing it, Ellen exclaimed, 'Ah, many's the time I've been *there*' before whisking the book away. In one of her footnotes Longley refers to Gladys's diaries, which contain many references to Ellen reading aloud to the girls but never once from Dickens. There are also mentions of Gladys taking visitors to the nearby Dickens Birthplace Museum (in Portsea, opened in 1904), but it seems that they were never once accompanied there by her mother.

Readers of Longley's article are given no information about how, when and why the Robinson family left Margate, or how they came to be living in the Berkshire village of Calcot in 1900 and later apparently somewhere near Portsea, a Portsmouth suburb. All this had been described in the final article of Morley's 'Theatrical Ternans' series (above, p. 141). This had introduced Canon Benham into the story, though without mentioning that he had once been a highly popular Vice-President of the Dickens Fellowship. Morley records Benham's celebrated 'Public Readings' from Dickens during his time as Vicar of Margate and his successful involvement of Ellen Robinson in this activity. He even mentions Ellen's giving Benham the pen Dickens had used to write *Drood* – though, of course, he carefully avoids any reference to the covering letter from Benham to Wright with its highly indiscreet postscript. Morley also briefly tells how the Robinsons had to give up the Margate school because of George's ill-health and how, after a short time running another school in London, they had unsuccessfully tried their hand at market-gardening at Calcot, just outside Reading. He summarises the later history of Ellen and her two sisters and describes how they all ended up living together first at Calcot and then later in Southsea. He also gives details of Geoffrey Robinson's not-undistinguished military career and his subsequent forays into bookselling and professional acting.

All this is dealt with in the later chapters of *A Pardoner's Tale* but is not detailed in Longley's 1985 *Dickensian* article. What emerges there very clearly is her desire that her readers should register a link between the last date on which Ellen can be traced as giving one of her celebrated Dickens readings and the date at which she is likely to have become aware, perhaps warned by

Georgina, that there was beginning to be a revival of the damaging gossip of 1858/59 about her relationship with Dickens as a result of Thomas Wright's 'sniffing around' (to recall the phrase used of Wright by Kate Perugini in a letter written about this time to George Bernard Shaw). The last public Dickens reading that Longley could trace was one given at Tilehurst Village Hall, Reading, in February 1897 which, she notes, was just a couple of months or so before Wright interviewed Benham. It seems more than likely that, as she suggests, Ellen's rigid silence about Dickens for the last fifteen or so years of her life, and her avoidance of anything connected with him, apart from her continued friendship with Georgina (Mamie had died in 1896), was the direct result of her alarm that the scandalmongering of nearly thirty years before seemed now about to erupt again with who knows what terrible effect upon her marriage, her children, her social life and standing.

There is also some evidence, mentioned by Longley in *A Pardoner's Tale* but not included in her *Dickensian* article, that Ellen had been prepared not only to give public Dickens readings in the years after his death but also to talk about him to Dickens enthusiasts. In his *Rambles in Dickens Land*, published in 1894, Robert Allbut wrote that 'a lady personally acquainted with the great novelist' had informed him 'that she was once taken by Mr Dickens to No. 10 Green Street', where he showed her the house, still a curiosity shop, which he had used for the home of Little Nell, 'pointing out an inner room . . . as her bedroom' and so on. Who could this lady have been but Ellen? She would, one imagines, have had a particular interest in seeing the home of her famous fictional namesake. Her anonymity was certainly safe with Allbut. When asked by a fellow-topographer in the November 1913 *Dickensian* to identify the lady in question, he firmly declined to do so in a letter published in the next issue: 'The information given', he wrote, 'was *strictly private.*'

The Dickensian is read only by Dickens enthusiasts and specialists. Despite Longley's monumental labours, therefore, Ellen was, at the beginning of the last decade of the twentieth century, still a very shadowy figure as far as the general reading public was concerned. One might have expected that during the great upsurge of feminist criticism and scholarship in the 1970s and early 1980s she would have become a prime target for researchers, given the way Dickens's male biographers had tended to marginalise her (Pope-Hennessy had been less inclined to do this) and to construct her identity in terms of certain of the novelist's later female characters. It was not until the later 1980s, however, that this situation changed. Ellen attracted the interest of the distinguished literary biographer Claire Tomalin, who had already published much-acclaimed lives of two feminist heroines, Mary Wollstonecraft and Katherine Mansfield. On 14 October 1990 readers of *The Independent on Sunday* opened their newspaper to find a two-page article by Tomalin with the headline 'A Tale of Two Nellies'. Beneath this there appeared a question hinting excitingly at some kind of conspiracy theory: 'If Charles Dickens loved Ellen Ternan, and his daughter Kate admired her, why have his biographers gone to such lengths to blacken her name?' Two accompanying illustrations show a rather wistful-looking young Ellen and the older Dickens very much in country-gentleman mode with his bowler hat somewhat rakishly tilted to one side and staring hard, not to say fiercely, at the camera. In the article, Tomalin summarises the history of the Ternan scandal from *This Side Idolatry* onwards. She draws attention to Longley's tireless campaign (which *Independent on Sunday* readers would have known nothing about) to clear Ellen's name and replace the depiction of her by Wright and by Edgar Johnson as cold, mercenary and capricious with the image of 'a warm-hearted, witty, intelligent woman, cultured and charming'. Tribute is paid to Longley's generosity in sharing her work with others, including Tomalin herself. Tomalin makes it clear, however, that she does not share Longley's view that Dickens's relationship with Ellen was platonic. Longley had not yet published her theory that the close association of Ellen with Dickens was partly owing to the fact that she and her mother might have been using their professional skills to help him with voice production for his public readings: her 'Ellen Ternan: Muse of the Readings?' appeared in the summer 1991 issue of *The Dickensian*. Tomalin, however, had read her arguments in favour of this idea in *A Pardoner's Tale* and had found them unconvincing. She alludes to them in her *Independent on Sunday* article, making the idea seem – no doubt inadvertently – rather more strained than it actually is by referring to 'elocution lessons' rather than to voice production.

Tomalin's book *The Invisible Woman: The Story of Ellen Ternan and Charles Dickens* was dedicated to Longley, who is also warmly thanked in the Acknowledgements. It was published on 31 October 1990 to universally enthusiastic reviews, became an instant best-seller and went on to win no fewer than three major literary prizes. It opens with a striking evocation of the world of early nineteenth-century English provincial theatre, to which Ellen's maternal grandmother and her mother both belonged. The subsequent account of Dickens and Ellen's relationship insofar as it is known is solidly based on all the relevant scholarly research. Whenever she ventures beyond this, Tomalin's imagined sequence of events is generally plausible, neither straining nor contradicting such actual evidence as we have, even though it can only be speculative – see, for example, her version of what occurred between Dickens and Ellen at Doncaster in September 1857: 'Either Ellen's own manner or a warning from her mother made [Dickens] draw back from his headlong wooing and understand that she and her sisters were not easy game.' The fact is that we simply do not know why he left Doncaster a day earlier than he intended; we know only that he did so. The Pilgrim Editors have a note at this point in their volume VIII (1995) that seems merely to echo Tomalin: Dickens, they suggest, was 'perhaps discouraged by the Ternans from staying longer'.

Tomalin does seem to be the first investigator of this matter to suggest, surely correctly, that the urgent remonstrances sent to Dickens by both Wills and Forster in January 1859, and – surprisingly – included by Lehmann in his 1912 *Charles Dickens as Editor*, almost certainly relate to a wildly indiscreet idea Dickens had of letting Tavistock House on a long lease to the Ternans. But in her chapter 'Vanishing into Space', dealing with the years 1862–65, she has, like everyone else, to fall back upon speculation as to just exactly what was going on in Dickens's life during those years. Was Ellen living with her mother and if so *where* were they living – assuming that they were, in fact, living together as seems most likely? Since Carlton's Condette discoveries it has been generally assumed that they were living in France, which would account for Dickens's frequent cross-Channel trips at this time. Tomalin follows this assumption but has perforce to leave it an open question as to whether or not it was during this period that Ellen gave birth to that elusive male child said to have died in infancy. There is, Tomalin says, 'no hard evidence' for such an event, but on the other hand there is, she believes, too much of what she calls 'soft evidence' for the idea 'to be brushed aside entirely'.

The remainder of Part Two of *The Invisible Woman* deals with the later years of Ellen's relationship with Dickens, her story being deftly interwoven with the fascinating lives of her spirited sisters Fanny and Maria and their respective – very different – marriages. Tomalin describes Dickens's commuting to Slough, but in envisaging Ellen as mistress of Elizabeth Cottage 'Marianalike awaiting the visits of her Mr Tringham' she overlooks Longley's published discovery of the Church Street cottage. Like

Aylmer, she canvasses the possibility that yet another (this time very short-lived!) child was born at this time, focusing like him on two suggestive words in the diary: 'Arrival' on 13 April and 'Loss' on 20 April. A rather less sensational explanation of the latter word, at least, was to appear nine years later in volume XI of the Pilgrim Edition of Dickens's letters. This includes a letter from him dated 20 April 1867 to the Station Master at Paddington about the loss of a small bag he had been carrying.

Tomalin suggests likely reasons for the choice of Peckham as a suitable location for Dickens's ménage with Ellen (e.g., the new fast rail link with Waterloo) and, in the last chapter of this section, imagines what Ellen's sequestered existence may have been like during the last two years of Dickens's continuingly hectic life. Though living 'the classic role of the Fallen Woman', she must, Tomalin believes, have for much of the time 'endured the drearier aspects of both domesticity and daughterhood, an outcast of the outer suburbs'. She includes a piquant new anecdote about Dickens buying 'six pairs of ladies' silk stockings' at a mercer's shop in Hull when he was in that city to give a reading in 1869. This had been communicated to her by descendants of Edward Long, the young shop assistant who had served Dickens and to whom he had given a ticket for that evening's reading. The event was recalled in Long's obituary notice in the *Hull Daily Mail* in 1927 quoted by Tomalin in a footnote. It ends as follows: 'One thing he [Long] was never able to understand: why Dickens was buying ladies' stockings.' The date of this obituary is worth noting. One year later, after the furore that followed the publication of *This Side Idolatry*, it would have been simply impossible for this anecdote to have been published in a daily paper without being seen as highly suggestive. It is certainly so seen today in some not unexpected quarters: *The Sun* ran an interview with Tomalin about her new biography of Dickens on 12 October 2011 and informed its readers on the basis of this anecdote that 'Dickens used his trips outside London to secretly buy his teen conquest saucy black underwear'.

The later chapters of *The Invisible Woman* deal with the chequered lives of Ellen and her sisters after Dickens's death. Three lively and variously talented young women, bound together by close ties of sisterly affection and married to three very different husbands, are shown making their individual ways in the world. Ellen's devotion to her two children, especially to Geoffrey, comes across strongly. The last chapter of the book deals poignantly with the clearly devastating effect upon him of his discovery after Ellen's death that his adored mother was at least ten years older than she had given herself out to be, and that, on the word of no less a personage than Sir Henry Dickens himself, she had also been Charles Dickens's mistress. On the vexed question of just exactly what it was that Ellen told Benham about her connection with Dickens, and how trustworthy Wright's report of this is, Tomalin accepts that Benham said just what Wright reports him as saying (with 'intimacy' being understood to mean 'sexual intimacy') and her comment that this was 'not good behaviour in a clergyman' may strike us as being decidedly on the mild side in the circumstances. Her final chapter sums up the arguments for and against believing that Dickens and Ellen were lovers and concludes that, in the absence of verifiable facts, we can only fall back on personal judgment. And this is what she herself does when she writes that to her it seems, in the light of all she has read, 'most likely that it was so'.

The Invisible Woman was greeted with special enthusiasm by feminist scholars and has indeed become something of a feminist classic. The excitement its publication generated was renewed and increased the following year when it was published in paperback. This edition featured a new postscript with the title 'The Death of Dickens' which was trailed in *The Independent* on 21 September 1991 in a piece headed 'Charles Dickens's Last

Secret?' This related to another family tradition connected with Dickens that had been communicated to Tomalin. This time, however, it was one based wholly on hearsay and was a good deal more sensational in nature than the anecdote about his purchase of those ladies' silk stockings. It derived ultimately from a certain Rev. J. Chetwode Postans, who in 1872 had been minister of Linden Grove Congregational Church, just across the road from Windsor Lodge. According to Mr Postans, his church caretaker had one day told him, seemingly out of the blue, that Dickens had not died at Gad's Hill as so memorably described in the last volume of Forster's biography, published in 1874, but at another house 'in compromising circumstances'. The caretaker refused to say where this other house was but did say that he personally had been involved in secretly moving the body to Gad's Hill 'to avoid scandal'. This remarkable anecdote was related by Mr Postans to his son-in-law whose surname was Leeson and who later told *his* son. In 1959 this latter Mr Leeson wrote about it to *The Sunday Times* after that paper's publication of Aylmer's article claiming to have discovered Dickens and Ellen's illegitimate child. (The Leesons had apparently been unaware of any Dickens connection with Peckham before this.) Aylmer, to whom *The Sunday Times* passed Leeson's letter, had evidently been too preoccupied with the collapse of his 'discovery' of Ellen's and Dickens's supposed love-child to do much about it. There the matter rested, therefore, until all the publicity attendant on the publication of *The Invisible Woman* prompted J. C. Leeson, great-grandson of the Rev. Mr Postans, to contact Tomalin.

Forster's *Life* provides a moving account of Dickens's death at Gad's Hill. For the details Forster relied on Georgina, who was alone with Dickens at the time, Forster himself being away in Cornwall. Georgina, Tomalin believes, could and would have lied to save Dickens's reputation if he had indeed died, or become mortally ill, while with Ellen in Peckham. She thinks also that Ellen might have been prompt and resourceful enough to organise the removal of the dead or dying man from Peckham to Gad's Hill, a distance of twenty-four miles. Ellen *could* have hired a closed carriage and got the stricken man into it with the help of the church caretaker and the driver. She *could* have alerted Georgina to the situation by telegraphing the bad news to her at Gad's Hill, thus giving her time to get all the servants out of the way and be ready at the front door to receive Ellen and the dead or dying Dickens (on this point David Parker pertinently remarks in an article in the 2008 *Dickens Quarterly* that wording the telegram in such a way as to avoid arousing the suspicions of the clerk handling it would surely have been a tricky business). Tomalin develops a thrilling scenario – 'the unconscious man, the terrified, watchful woman, the carriage, coachman and horse steadily moving along roads so familiar to Dickens', etc. – for which she discovers some possible evidence through her close study of the records of Dickens's last day. Dickens, we know, had a substantial amount of cash on him early on the day of his death, but very little was found in his pockets when he died. How, Tomalin asks, can this be explained if the received version of his last day – that is Georgina's, which has him passing the whole day quietly at Gad's Hill – is correct? Might the discrepancy not be accounted for by the expenses Ellen would have incurred in organising his removal to Gad's Hill?

In the end, Tomalin does not unambiguously endorse this dramatic version of Dickens's death but leaves it as an open question. The final volume of the Pilgrim Edition of Dickens's letters, published in 2002, might have produced some new evidence, one way or the other, about the circumstances of Dickens's death but did not do so. Its editor, Graham Storey, merely footnotes the Leeson story as 'an oral tradition that queries the version of Dickens's death given by Georgina Hogarth and Forster'. In her biography *Charles Dickens: A Life* (2011)

Tomalin notes that no new information about this matter has come to light since 1991 and comments, 'I accept that it seems an unlikely story, although not an impossible one, given what we know of Dickens's habits [a reference, presumably, to his regular visits to Ellen in Peckham]'. She was less guarded in a pre-publication interview published in *The Observer* on 25 September 2011 when she was quoted as speaking of 'Dickensians' who have 'never liked the stuff I suggested about Dickens's death' and adding, 'But I haven't changed my mind. I'm sticking to it.'

The veracity of this odd story thus continues to remain entirely dependent on the bald assertion of one long-dead witness as passed down from one generation to another in a particular family. There can be no doubt, however, that following the wide publicity given to it by Tomalin, this more thrilling version of Dickens's death has caught the public's imagination and will continue, as the saying goes, to run and run.

Katharine Longley's last publication on Dickens appeared in the summer 1992 issue of *The Dickensian*. In it she re-examines the July 1867–July 1870 entries for 16 Linden Grove (Windsor Lodge) in the Peckham rate-books as published by Thomas Wright in his *Autobiography* (see above, p. 92). This is the sole surviving record of these entries, the rate-books themselves having been sent for salvage during World War II. Longley's scrutiny leads her to question the assumption that Ellen was living continuously at Windsor Lodge as Dickens's unofficial wife from June or July 1867 to June 1870, apart from the winter of 1867/8 when he was reading in America and she was visiting her sister Fanny Trollope in Florence. Mrs Ternan and Ellen had, Longley surmises, been living for six months at Windsor Lodge in July 1867 when the rates were paid by 'Frances Turnham', a common misspelling of Mrs Ternan's name. Succeeding half-year entries, from January 1868 onwards, show that Dickens himself was the ratepayer using his Tringham alias and having, Longley suggests, taken over the tenancy from Mrs Ternan. By 15 October 1868 Mrs Ternan can be found living at No. 32 Harrington Square, Hampstead Road, and Longley makes the reasonable presumption that Ellen was still living with her mother as she had been at Church Cottage in Slough. Longley's new discovery is that from mid-December 1868 to 12 June 1869 Mrs Ternan and Ellen were living in a furnished apartment at 10 Bath Place in Worthing; during this period their names appear regularly in the list of visitors to the resort published weekly in *The Worthing Intelligencer*. We know that during this time Dickens himself was away in Scotland, Ireland and the provinces on his Farewell Reading Tour which had begun in early October. At intervals he returned to read in London and at such times, presumably, Ellen might perhaps have made the occasional journey up to Victoria to rendezvous with him, though Longley does not speculate about this. After a Christmas break at Gad's Hill Dickens resumed his tour until it was abruptly abandoned on 22 April at the insistence of his doctor, Frank Beard. He then stayed in London, no doubt dividing his time between his flat over the office of *All The Year Round* in Wellington Street and Peckham, recovering his health in time to become a London tour guide (with Georgina and Mamie staying with him at a West End hotel) for the visiting Fieldses before entertaining them for a week at Gad's Hill in early June.

Unfortunately, *The Worthing Intelligencer* ceased publication soon after June 1869, so it cannot be used to determine whether the Ternans were again in Worthing in 1870. Longley does, however, report having seen a letter of 28 June 1870, in private hands, written by Fanny Trollope to her stepdaughter in which she mentions that 'Ellen's riding master in Worthing is quite a character'. She speculates as to whether this might indicate Mrs Ternan and Ellen were spending another season in Worthing.

Earlier in 1870, she notes, Mrs Ternan, at least, was living in London as shown by a letter of 20 January 1870 from Thomas Trollope to his publisher asking him to send some proofs to him 'care of "Mrs Ternan, 305 Vauxhall Bridge Road"'. Was Ellen living with her? Longley believes that Sala may be hinting at her presence there in his obituary tribute to Dickens (see above, p. 34) when, in writing of Dickens's extensive London perambulations, he mentions him as having been seen 'pursuing the even tenor of his way up the Vauxhall-Bridge-Road'.

Longley is suggesting that, contrary to the established belief that Ellen kept house for Dickens at Windsor Lodge for most of the last three years of his life, she was, in fact, living elsewhere with her mother for a great deal of that time while Dickens used the place as a bolt-hole for his writing, very much as he had used Elizabeth Cottage in Slough and other rural retreats earlier in his life. However, there is also the, admittedly third-hand, evidence of Mrs Goldring, who worked for Dickens at Windsor Lodge to be taken into account (see above, p. 34). She was reported as having spoken about Dickens's 'unofficial wife . . . reputed to be a connection of Mr Trollope' who lived with him at the Lodge. It is therefore not clear whether, or to what extent, Ellen was the châtelaine of Windsor Lodge. As to the story of Dickens collapsing at the Lodge and a woman organising his removal from there, Longley suggests that, if anything like that ever happened, the woman in question might well have been a neighbour who was married to a relative of his cousin by marriage, George Frederick Lawrence. Thomas Wright's papers show that a certain Guy Buckeridge living in Linden Grove had informed him that Dickens's 'association with Laurence [sic]' who lived in Linden Grove was 'well known' locally.

Lastly, Longley reveals that the dying statement by Jane Brown, reported to Ley by Ellen's daughter and published by him in *The Dickensian* in 1937 (see above, p. 94) was, in fact, significantly altered by him. The dying Brown, according to this version, told her sisters that if asked, she would have been able to swear to Gladys Reece 'that her dear mother never was the mistress of Charles Dickens'. What she actually said is revealed by documents examined by Longley at the Dickens Museum. These show that Brown's words as reported to Ley actually were 'your dear mother never lived with Charles Dickens'. Longley offers this as another scrap of evidence against the idea that Ellen and Dickens ever co-habited in Windsor Lodge.

Since 1992 no further information shedding fresh light on Dickens's relationship with Ellen has surfaced, apart from a couple of items to be found in scholarly publications. In a footnote to volume IX of the Pilgrim Edition of Dickens's letters, published in 1997, the editors cite various payments to 'H P Trust', 'HP' and 'HPN' made at irregular intervals from Dickens's bank account at Coutts's after 23 May 1859 (there are also some less frequent payments marked 'Young Ladies Quarters'). The initials, they suggest, surely stand for 'Houghton Place' and 'Houghton Place Ellen'. Fanny and Maria Ternan, we recall, had bought Houghton Place in March 1859, presumably with funds supplied by Dickens, and made the house over to Ellen a year later on her twenty-first birthday. This must have been in accordance with Dickens's 'Plan B', so to speak, after he had been dissuaded from the huge indiscretion of letting Tavistock House to the Ternans on a long lease. The discovery of these payments would surely have been a gift to any alert and informed journalist in quest of a sensational Ellen-related 'Dickens story' who had troubled to work through the Pilgrim footnotes.

Similarly, any journalist trawling through *The Dickens Quarterly* for 2008 might have derived another good Dickens and Ellen story from Robert R. Garnett's revisiting of the matter first raised by William Kent in 1949 when he proposed that the unnamed fourteenth mourner at Dickens's funeral must have been Ellen (above, p. 108). Garnett shows that it was Wilkie Collins who supplied a report of the occasion to *The Times*, Forster being too exhausted and overcome to do so, and surmises that in the haste of compiling his report Collins failed to notice the discrepancy between the overall total of mourners and the number of those he actually named. The Dickens family, as well as Forster and Collins, would, of course, have been intensely concerned to keep Ellen's presence among the mourners utterly secret as part of the whole process of 'keeping up appearances'. Garnett argues very plausibly that Dickens himself took care to create the circumstances whereby Ellen, the great love of his later life, would be able to see him into his grave without scandal. It was, Garnett believes, the reason for his insistence in his will that his funeral should be conducted in a 'strictly private manner' with 'no public announcement' being made of the time of his burial and that the number of people attending should be limited to no more than 'three plain mourning coaches' would hold.

What Dickens biographers have long yearned for is some first-hand account of Dickens and Ellen together, how they customarily behaved towards each other, what they talked about, how they passed their time together, the nature of their domesticity if they did indeed ever co-habit. There is one time-honoured anecdote that has seemed to offer us such a glimpse, Andrew De Ternant's report of what he claims Francesco Berger had told him about those pleasant evenings that he, Berger, had spent in Mornington Crescent around 1859/60 taking a hand at cards with Dickens, Mrs Ternan and Ellen and later playing the piano to accompany Dickens and Ellen as they sang duets (see above, p. 86). De Ternant published this beguiling anecdote in *Notes and Queries* in 1933, just after Berger died. It was quoted two years later by Thomas Wright in his *Life of Dickens* and has featured in just about every Dickens biography since, including my own in 2009. Claire Tomalin, however, while working on her recent *Charles Dickens: A Life*, had the curiosity to research De Ternant and discovered that he was a notorious hoaxer who evidently delighted in getting phoney anecdotes, personally authenticated by himself, about recently dead composers and others published in *The Musical Times*, *Notes and Queries* and other specialist publications. It seems a good deal more than likely, therefore, that this charming vignette of Dickens, Ellen and her mother enjoying themselves at Houghton Place is apocryphal.

'Invisible' though she may have been at Dickens's funeral and in the received version of his life-story for more than sixty years afterwards, Ellen has now, thanks to Tomalin's 1990 best-seller, been a highly visible presence in the public's perception of Dickens's life-story for more than two decades. Simon Gray was inspired by Tomalin's work to make Ellen the convincingly conflicted heroine of his radio play *Little Nell*, broadcast on Radio 4 in 2006 and adapted by him for the stage the following year when it was directed, to considerable critical acclaim, by Peter Hall at the Theatre Royal, Bath. In 2008, as part of its 'Victorian Passions' season, BBC4 TV screened a documentary about Dickens and Ellen, with dramatised episodes: 'New docudrama lays bare Charles Dickens's obsession with a teenaged girl', *The Daily Telegraph* lip-smackingly reported on 16 June. Bizarrely, Ellen was shown in this programme as very visible indeed, standing anxiously and rather prominently in the wings at all Dickens's public readings; after one especially highly-charged performance of *Sikes and Nancy*, Dickens was shown stumbling off the stage and into her arms saying brokenly, 'Take me home!'

Two years after television viewers had been regaled with this bizarre production the BBC announced that it was planning to make a full-length feature film about Dickens and Ellen Ternan, a film that, *The Independent* reported on 18 May 2010, was 'set to expose' what it called 'this little-known aspect of Dickens's life, first documented in Claire Tomalin's revisionist biography'. Given the history of media fascination with this particular Victorian scandal, it seems only reasonable to assume that even this film will not be the last of such 'exposures'.

Will we ever know?

In this book I have been tracing the excitement in the media and elsewhere concerning the gradual uncovering of the great secret of the last twelve years of Dickens's life – his relationship with Ellen Ternan. The central mystery of the nature of this hidden relationship remains obscure but finds a ready focus in the question of sexuality. In his 1952 'Foreword' to Nisbet's *Dickens and Ellen Ternan* Edmund Wilson writes, 'The unprejudiced reader of Miss Nisbet's book will certainly come to the conclusion that, if Dickens's relations with Ellen were, as the Dickensians insist, Platonic, he was an even odder case than one had thought'. This was, no doubt, intended to be jovially dismissive of the said Dickensians as they stoutly upheld the purity and moral integrity of their hero against what they saw as the scandalmongering second-hand revelations of Wright and Storey. Today's Dickensians, however, even fully paid-up members of the Dickens Fellowship, do not generally take this line and I would guess that the number of those who still believe that Dickens's relationship with Ellen was indeed Platonic is not large.

There is, moreover, much greater recognition now among all Dickens's readers, both inside and outside the Fellowship, of just how odd a case he actually was and nowhere more so than in his relations with women. His connection with Ellen has been seen by many as very much part and parcel of this oddity. It has been linked, for example, with the extraordinary and long-lasting intensity of his response to the sudden death of his beloved sister-in-law Mary Hogarth at the age of seventeen, which was just Ellen's age when he first met her. Peter Ackroyd makes this connection when he argues in his acclaimed 1990 biography *Dickens* that, since Dickens's 'behaviour was always quite exceptional, we should not fall into the trap of expecting him to behave in a conventional way with Ellen'. To Ackroyd it seems 'almost inconceivable that theirs was in any sense a "consummated" affair' and he argues persuasively that their relationship acted for Dickens as 'the realisation of one of his most enduring fictional fantasies', namely 'that of sexless marriage with a young, idealised virgin'. In the same year that his *Dickens* appeared, however, Claire Tomalin published *The Invisible Woman*, at the end of which, having carefully sifted all the evidence assembled over the years by Katharine Longley and others, and having made full allowance for Dickens being 'an extraordinary man in many respects', she concludes that, in the light of all that she has read, it seems to her 'most likely' that he and Ellen were lovers.

Since 1990 no new evidence has come to light that might help definitively to solve this mystery. Indeed, the only evidence that could do so would be either the discovery of a letter or letters from Dickens to Ellen, or from Ellen to him, that made clear the nature of their relationship, or the discovery of a birth certificate or other documentary evidence of the existence of the son that Kate Perugini and Henry Dickens both believed to have been born to their father and Ellen. As far as letters are concerned, we can be pretty certain that all those that Dickens ever received from Ellen would have been incinerated in the regular bonfires of his correspondence that he made from 1860 onwards. As for his own letters written to his 'dear girl', Kate Perugini seemed to have believed that they might not have been destroyed. In her correspondence with George Bernard Shaw in December 1897 (above, p. 82) about her late mother's hoard of letters from Dickens, she makes thrilling mention of 'other letters in which the real man is revealed, minus his Sunday clothes and all shams, and with his heart and soul burning like jewels in a dark place'. It is, of course, always possible that Dickens's letters to Ellen were *not* destroyed and that there may actually be some truth in the strange anecdote related by Thomas Wright that we have noticed above (p. 87) about their being offered for sale to the Dickensian enthusiast W. R. Hughes some time around 1893. However, given the lengths to which Ellen went after 1870 to re-invent herself and radically to revise the history of her connection with Dickens, it seems unlikely in the extreme that she would have preserved his letters to her, whatever Kate may have believed.

As to the evidence for a child having been born to Dickens and Ellen and dying in infancy, other students of Dickens biography have followed Carlton in focussing on various strangely agitated, occasionally inconsistent and evasive, elements in Dickens's letters of 1862–63, letters that in the years since Carlton wrote have been collected and annotated in detail in the Pilgrim Edition of Dickens's Letters. In his preface to volume X of this Edition (1998), covering the years 1862 to 1864, Graham Storey comments that certain letters 'point strongly to some crisis centred on Ellen in January 1863; probably an illness, just possibly a pregnancy'. These letters show Dickens making frequent cross-Channel trips during the period and contain references by him to 'some rather miserable anxieties', 'sundry ties and troubles' which cause him to 'oscillate' between England and France, and so on. He refers also to an unnamed 'sick friend' in France about whom he is anxious and whom he has to go and see.

Foremost among recent investigators of these letters have been John Bowen, now Professor of English at York University, and the American scholar Professor Robert Garnett, whose article on Ellen's presence at Dickens's funeral has already been noticed. In his fascinating article in the Winter 2000 issue of *The Dickensian* Bowen connects the letters and Dickens's cross-Channel expeditions of 1862–63 with a story called 'His Boots' that Dickens wrote for the 1862 Christmas Number of *All The Year Round*. This story, set in a provincial town in northern France, centres on a pretty little female child called Bebelle who, it is made clear, is illegitimate. It describes how Bebelle comes to be adopted by an initially morosely indifferent middle-aged Englishman who has come abroad after repudiating his own daughter for having an illegitimate child. 'His Boots', Bowen comments, is 'a fantasy of adoption and a story about the possible fates of illegitimate children' and he notes a curious reference back to it in a letter Dickens wrote to Wills in June 1864 when he was planning the next *All The Year Round* Christmas Number. Telling Wills that his 'present Mysterious Disappearance' is in the direction of France, Dickens says that he seems 'to have a sort of inspiration' for the Number 'that may blend the undiminished attractions of Mrs Lirriper [narrator and heroine of the hugely popular Christmas Number for 1863] with those of the Bebelle life in Paris'. Bowen persuasively suggests that, since Bebelle herself does not appear in the 1864 Number, the phrase 'the Bebelle life' (left unannotated by the Pilgrim Editors) may well, like 'Mysterious Disappearance', be a code used between Dickens and Wills to stand for something in Dickens's life that could not be directly named, in this case, so Bowen believes, the short-lived child Ellen bore him in France.

A few years after Bowen's article appeared Robert Garnett subjected the 1862–63 letters to close scrutiny in *The Dickens Quarterly* (September 2006). He constructs a plausible scenario involving Ellen's hasty removal to France, most probably accompanied by her mother, in the summer of 1862, after discovering she was pregnant, and subsequent visits to her made by Dickens in the late summer and autumn. His cross-Channel trips culminated in October in a three-month stay in a Paris hotel where he was accompanied by Mamie and Georgina. Like some earlier scholars, Garnett suggests there may have been some connection between the mysterious heart complaint from which Georgina suffered during the summer and autumn of 1862, causing Dickens great concern, and her emotional and psychological response to an Ellen pregnancy. Dickens returned to Gad's Hill with Mamie and Georgina for Christmas. He then went back to France alone, remaining there for some weeks – perhaps, Garnett suggests, in order to be on hand for a birth expected to take place in January or February. If Ellen did indeed give birth at this time, she would most likely have done so in the anonymity of Paris rather than in some provincial town or village, but since all records of births, marriages and deaths were destroyed during the Paris Commune of 1871, actual documentary proof of such a birth is unlikely ever to be discovered. Garnett also draws attention to the later letter of 9 April in which Dickens refers to 'a hasty summons to attend upon a sick friend' that obliges him to 'prepare for a rush across the Channel'. Again plausibly, he suggests that this might well relate to an emergency resulting from the child having died just as both Kate Perugini and Sir Henry Dickens had told Storey that it did.

The Garnett hypothesis, so to call it, is, I think, probably as close as we will ever get to solving the mystery of the nature of Dickens's relationship with Ellen, at least during the early 1860s. Whether they continued to be lovers after that, whether they ever actually co-habited in Condette or Peckham or elsewhere, whether there was, in fact, another child who did survive (which possibility allows us to entertain the exciting idea that there might, as Aylmer and others have sometimes believed, be some 'Fitz-Dickenses', so to speak, extant among us today): these are questions unlikely now ever to be resolved. But even if they were to be, the Great Charles Dickens Scandal would, I believe, lose none of its interest for the media and for the public at large, since one of the main things that Dickens still represents in our culture is an ideal of perfect, blissful, quintessentially English, domesticity. Contributing to the 2008 BBC television programme *Dickens' Secret Lover*, Professor Kathryn Hughes memorably remarked that if the fact that Dickens had a sexual liaison with Ellen could be proved beyond all reasonable doubt, the effect upon the public mind would 'be like finding that Father Christmas has been to a brothel'. It does indeed seem that the frisson and fascination we find in this topic, inspiring the kind of newspaper headlines quoted in my Introduction, are destined to remain with us indefinitely.

Dickens's Personal Statement, 1858

Three-and-twenty years have passed since I entered on my present relations with the Public. They began when I was so young, that I find them to have existed for nearly a quarter of a century.

Through all that time I have tried to be as faithful to the Public, as they have been to me. It was my duty never to trifle with them, or deceive them, or presume upon their favor, or do any thing with it but work hard to justify it. I have always endeavoured to discharge that duty.

My conspicuous position has often made me the subject of fabulous stories and unaccountable statements. Occasionally, such things have chafed me, or even wounded me; but, I have always accepted them as the shadows inseparable from the light of my notoriety and success. I have never obtruded any such personal uneasiness of mine, upon the generous aggregate of my audience.

For the first time in my life, and I believe for the last, I now deviate from the principle I have so long observed, by presenting myself in my own Journal in my own private character, and entreating all my brethren (as they deem that they have reason to think well of me, and to know that I am a man who has ever been unaffectedly true to our common calling), to lend their aid to the dissemination of my present words.

Some domestic trouble of mine, of long-standing, on which I will make no further remark than that it claims to be respected, as being of a sacredly private nature, has lately been brought to an arrangement, which involves no anger or ill-will of any kind, and the whole origin, progress, and surrounding circumstances of which have been, throughout, within the knowledge of my children. It is amicably composed, and its details have now but to be forgotten by those concerned in it.

By some means, arising out of wickedness, or out of folly, or out of inconceivable wild chance, or out of all three, this trouble has been made the occasion of misrepresentations, most grossly false, most monstrous, and most cruel – involving, not only me, but innocent persons dear to my heart, and innocent persons of whom I have no knowledge, if, indeed, they have any existence – and so widely spread, that I doubt if one reader in a thousand will peruse these lines, by whom some touch of the breath of these slanders will not have passed, like an unwholesome air.

Those who know me and my nature, need no assurance under my hand that such calumnies are as irreconcileable with me, as they are, in their frantic incoherence, with one another. But, there is a great multitude who know me through my writings, and who do not know me otherwise; and I cannot bear that one of them should be left in doubt, or hazard of doubt, through my poorly shrinking from taking the unusual means to which I now resort, of circulating the Truth.

I most solemnly declare, then – and this I do, both in my own name and in my wife's name – that all the lately whispered rumours touching the trouble at which I have glanced, are abominably false. And that whosoever repeats one of them after this denial, will lie as wilfully and as foully as it is possible for any false witness to lie, before Heaven and earth.

CHARLES DICKENS
[*The Times*, 7 June 1858]

The 'Violated Letter'

TAVISTOCK HOUSE, TAVISTOCK SQUARE, LONDON, W.C.

Tuesday, 25th May, 1858

MY DEAR ARTHUR, – You have not only my full permission to show this, but I beg you to show, to any one who wishes to do me right, or to any one who may have been misled into doing me wrong.

Faithfully yours.

TAVISTOCK HOUSE, TAVISTOCK SQUARE, LONDON, W.C.

[Enclosure]   Tuesday, May 25, 1858

Mrs Dickens and I have lived unhappily together for many years. Hardly any one who has known us intimately can fail to have known that we are, in all respects of character and temperament, wonderfully unsuited to each other. I suppose that no two people, not vicious in themselves, ever were joined together, who had a greater difficulty in understanding one another, or who had less in common. An attached woman servant (more friend to both of us than a servant), who lived with us sixteen years, and is now married, and who was, and still is in Mrs Dickens's confidence and in mine, who had the closest familiar experience of this unhappiness, in London, in the country, in France, in Italy, wherever we have been, year after year, month after month, week after week, day after day, will bear testimony to this.

Nothing has, on many occasions, stood between us and a separation but Mrs Dickens's sister, Georgina Hogarth. From the age of fifteen, she has devoted herself to our house and our children. She has been their playmate, nurse, instructress, friend, protectress, adviser and companion. In the manly consideration toward Mrs Dickens which I owe to my wife, I will merely remark of her that the peculiarity of her character has thrown all the children on some one else. I do not know – I cannot by any stretch of fancy imagine – what would have become of them but for this aunt, who has grown up with them, to whom they are devoted, and who has sacrificed the best part of her youth and life to them.

She has remonstrated, reasoned, suffered and toiled, again and again to prevent a separation between Mrs Dickens and me. Mrs Dickens has often expressed to her her sense of her affectionate care and devotion in the house – never more strongly than within the last twelve months.

For some years past Mrs Dickens has been in the habit of representing to me that it would be better for her to go away and live apart; that her always increasing estrangement made a mental disorder under which she sometimes labours – more, that she felt herself unfit for the life she had to lead as my wife, and that she would be better far away. I have uniformly replied that we must bear our misfortune, and fight the fight out to the end; that the children were the first consideration, and that I feared they must bind us together 'in appearance'.

At length, within these three weeks, it was suggested to me by Forster that even for their sakes, it would surely be better to reconstruct and rearrange their unhappy home. I empowered him to treat with Mrs Dickens, as the friend of both of us for one and twenty years. Mrs Dickens wished to add on her part, Mark Lemon, and did so. On Saturday last Lemon wrote to Forster that Mrs Dickens 'gratefully and thankfully accepted' the terms I proposed to her.

Of the pecuniary part of them, I will only say that I believe they are as generous as if Mrs Dickens were a lady of distinction and I a man of fortune. The remaining parts of them are easily described – my eldest boy to live with Mrs Dickens and take care of her; my eldest girl to keep my house; both my girls, and all my children but the eldest son, to live with me, in the continued companionship of their aunt Georgina, for whom they have all the tenderest affection that I have ever seen among young people, and who has a higher claim (as I have often declared for many years) upon my affection, respect and gratitude than anybody in this world.

I hope that no one who may become acquainted with what I write here, can possibly be so cruel and unjust, as to put any misconstruction on our separation, so far. My elder children all understand it perfectly, and all accept it as inevitable. There is not a shadow of doubt or concealment among us – my eldest son and I are one, as to it all.

Two wicked persons who should have spoken very differently of me, in consideration of earned respect and gratitude, have (as I am told, and indeed to my personal knowledge) coupled with this separation the name of a young lady for whom I have a great attachment and regard. I will not repeat her name – I honour it too much. Upon my soul and honour, there is not on this earth a more virtuous and spotless creature than that young lady. I know her to be innocent and pure, and as good as my own dear daughters. Further, I am quite sure that Mrs Dickens, having received this assurance from me, must now believe it, in the respect I know her to have for me, and in the perfect confidence I know her in her better moments to repose in my truthfulness.

On this head, again, there is not a shadow of doubt or concealment between my children and me. All is open and plain among us, as though we were brothers and sisters. They are perfectly certain that I would not deceive them, and the confidence among us is without a fear.

29th May, 1858

It having been stated to us that in reference to the differences which have resulted in the separation of Mr and Mrs Charles Dickens, certain statements have been circulated that such differences are occasioned by circumstances deeply affecting the moral character of Mr Dickens and compromising the reputation and good name of others, we solemnly declare that we now disbelieve such statements. We know that they are not believed by Mrs Dickens, and we pledge ourselves on all occasions to contradict them, as entirely destitute of foundation.

[*Here follow the signatures of Mrs Hogarth and her youngest daughter.*]

Text from Nonesuch *Letters*, vol. 3, pp. 21–3.

Who's Who

I have included here those members of the Dickens and Ternan families who are most relevant to this book, also the most important figures – biographers, independent scholars, and members of the Dickens Fellowship – in the history of the Dickens Scandal. Modern (post-1960) biographers of Dickens and professional academics who are all sufficiently identified in the text and whose works are given in the Bibliography are not listed. *ODNB* = *The Oxford Dictionary of National Biography*.

ALYMER, Sir Felix (1898–1979), for many years a leading member of the theatrical profession, was knighted in 1965. Having become fascinated at an early age by attempts to complete *The Mystery of Edwin Drood*, he contributed two articles entitled 'The Drood Case Reopened' to *The Dickensian* in 1924 and 1925. His *Dickens Incognito* (1959) was followed by *The Drood Case* in 1964. He was elected a Vice-President of the Dickens Fellowship in 1951. See *ODNB*.

BECHHOFER ROBERTS, Carl Eric (1894–1949), had written a number of books about India and Russia, based on his travels in those countries, as well as biographies of Winston Churchill, and of Lord Birkenhead, whose private secretary he was for six years, before he published his sensational novel about Dickens in 1928. He was a staffer on *The Daily Express* from 1926 to 1929 and continued to be a prolific author in various genres until, like Sir Henry Dickens, he met his death in a traffic accident.

BENHAM, Canon William (1831–1910), was Vicar of Margate 1872–80 and from 1882 Rector of the City of London church of St Edmund the King, Lombard Street. A voluminous contributor to religious literature and co-author of a biography of Archbishop Tait (1891), he also edited the poetry and the letters of William Cowper and was an admirer of Thomas Wright's biography of the poet. An ardent Dickensian, Benham was for many years an active and highly popular member of the Dickens Fellowship, of which he was a Vice-President. He contributed the Dickens chapters to *Memorials of Kent* (1909). See *ODNB*.

CARLTON, William J. (1886–1973), began his career in publishing in 1902 and, after service in the First World War, worked for the International Labour Office from 1921. He became Librarian in 1940 and retired in 1946. He achieved distinction as a historian of shorthand and published his *Charles Dickens, Shorthand Writer* in 1926. As a result of his outstanding gift for painstaking and meticulous research, he became a leading authority on Dickens's early life and after his retirement contributed many important articles to *The Dickensian* which added considerably to our knowledge of Dickens. The Editors of the Pilgrim Edition of Dickens's letters acknowledge a great indebtedness to his work.

DEXTER, Walter (1877–1944), a businessman, was editor of, and a prolific contributor to, *The Dickensian* between 1925 and 1944. He was the author of several works of Dickensian topography and an indefatigable editor of Dickens's letters, large numbers of which he published for the first time in *The Dickensian*. He edited various volumes of Dickens's correspondence with individual people, including his letters to Catherine (*Mr and Mrs Charles Dickens: His Letters to Her*, 1935) and also edited the three substantial volumes of letters that form part of the Nonesuch Dickens, published in 1938.

DICKENS, Sir Henry Fielding (1849–1933), Dickens's eighth child and sixth son, was the most successful of all Dickens's children. He studied law at Cambridge and was called to the bar in 1873, became Common Serjeant of the City of London in 1917, and was knighted in 1922. He was President of the Dickens Fellowship 1903–1910 and thereafter Life President. He was famous as a public reader from his father's works to raise money for good causes. His memoirs entitled *The Recollections of Sir Henry Dickens, K.C.* were published posthumously in 1934 and incorporated his earlier *Memories of My Father* (1928).

DICKENS, Mary ('Mamie') (1838–1896), Dickens's third child and eldest daughter, chose never to marry. She remained with her father after his separation from her mother, running his household for him in conjunction with her aunt Georgina Hogarth. Her life after Dickens's death was consecrated to perpetuating and celebrating his memory in various ways. With her aunt she worked on an edition of his letters and until 1876 shared a home with her. She then went to live with the family of an Anglican clergyman in Manchester to help him in his philanthropic work among the poor. In 1895, despite declining health, she wrote a loving memoir, *My Father As I Recall Him*, very much presenting Dickens as a great and good man, 'one apart from all other beings', and a kind and loving father. She was, however, too ill to correct the proofs and died shortly before the book's publication.

HOGARTH, Georgina (1827–1917), was the eighth child of George Hogarth, Dickens's father-in-law. She became a member of the Dickens household in 1842, helping Catherine with the children, and stayed with Dickens, running his household in conjunction with his elder daughter Mamie, after he ended his marriage in 1858. Together with Mamie she edited successive volumes of Dickens's letters after his death, kept in touch with all her nephews and nieces, also with Ellen Robinson and her family, and was a vigilant 'Guardian of the Beloved Memory', much venerated by the Dickens Fellowship. See *ODNB*.

KITTON, Frederic George (1856–1904), was born in Norwich. He early showed himself to be a talented wood-engraver and provided numerous illustrations for *The Graphic*, also for W. R. Hughes's *A Week's Tramp in Dickens-Land* (1891). He revered Dickens and was an indefatigable researcher into all aspects of his life and work, and wrote extensively on the subject. He was a founder member of the Dickens Fellowship and would have been the first Editor of its journal *The Dickensian* had it not been for his untimely death. See *ODNB*.

LEY, J. W. T. (1878–1943), was a professional journalist who became President of the National Union of Journalists in 1939. A keen Dickensian from an early age, he published *The Dickens Circle* in 1918 and ten years later came his monumental anno-tated edition of Forster's *Life of Dickens*, which remains the standard scholarly edition in use today. He was a prolific contributor to *The Dickensian* and a tireless opponent of Thomas

Wright and others who claimed that the relationship between Dickens and Ellen Ternan had been a sexual one.

LONGLEY, Katharine M. (1920–2009), was an archivist at York Minster until her retirement in 1983 and a noted authority on Recusant history. In 1966 she published a biography of St Margaret Clitherow under the pseudonym of Mary Claridge. Her keen interest in detective fiction attracted her to Dickens's unsolved mystery story of *Edwin Drood* and she wrote an ending to it called 'The Whispering Reed' (unpublished). As a result of her friendship with Helen Wickham, a lifelong friend of Ellen Robinson's daughter Gladys, she became deeply interested in the subject of Ellen's relationship with Dickens and wrote a long, very thoroughly researched, study of the subject entitled 'A Pardoner's Tale' which remains unpublished.

MORLEY, Malcolm (1890–1966), was an actor, producer and theatre manager. He was associated with the management of the Everyman Theatre, Hampstead, from 1926 to 1931 and managed the Canadian Repertory Co. in Ottawa 1947–50. He was a noted theatre historian, his publications including *The Old Marylebone Theatre* (1960) and *The Royal West London Theatre* (1962). For *The Dickensian* he wrote between 1947 and 1955 a series of articles dealing comprehensively with contemporary stage adaptations of Dickens's writings as well as another series, 'The Theatrical Ternans' (see Bibliography).

PERUGINI, Kate (1839–1929), Dickens's second daughter, nick-named 'Lucifer-Box' by her father on account of her fiery temperament. In 1860 she married the artist Charles Collins, brother of Wilkie. She herself became a noted artist specialising in portraits of children and exhibited at the Royal Academy. Collins died in 1873 and the following year Kate married another artist, Carlo Perugini, by whom she had a son who died in infancy. In 1906 she published some tender reminiscences of her father's last days in *The Pall Mall Magazine*, but evidently in her extreme old age spoke rather differently about him to Gladys Storey.

ROBINSON, Ellen Lawless (Nelly) née TERNAN (1839–1914), the youngest daughter of Thomas and Frances Eleanor Ternan, was born in Rochester at the home of her uncle William Ternan. Her middle name derived from her paternal grandmother's father, a Dublin brewer. She made her stage début in Sheffield at the age of three and, both before and after her father's death in 1846, she toured the country with the rest of her family. She made her London début in 1857, the year she met Dickens, and acted with his Amateur Company, together with her mother and sister Maria. She retired from the stage two years later, never having made much mark as an actress. In 1876, six years after Dickens's death, having deducted ten years from her actual age, she married George Wharton Robinson and worked with him in running a boys' school in Margate. The Robinsons had two children, Geoffrey and Gladys. In 1886 George's poor health necessitated his giving up the school, after which the family's fortunes seem somewhat to have declined. George died in 1907 and Ellen's last years were passed in Southsea, where she shared a house with her two sisters.

STOREY, Gladys, O.B.E. (1886–1978), was the daughter of George Augustus Storey, R.A. In the 1920s she and her mother became close friends of Kate Perugini, making regular weekly visits to her in her Chelsea flat. In 1929 she published a volume of memoirs called *All Sorts of People* recounting her brief career on the West End stage and also her recruiting activities in World War I when she became the only female 'Recruiting Sergeant' officially attached to the War Office. She describes also her successful campaign to arrange for tins of Bovril to be delivered to all front-line troops, a campaign that she re-activated in World War II and for which she was awarded the Order of the British Empire.

TAYLOR, Maria Susanna née TERNAN (1837–1904), was the middle daughter of Frances and Thomas Ternan. She made her first appearance on stage at the age of three and early on developed a distinct talent for comedy. She played with Charles Kean at the Princess's Theatre 1854–7 before acting with her mother and Ellen in Dickens's Amateur Company. She subsequently consolidated her London reputation as an excellent comic actress. In 1863 she married an Oxford brewer William Taylor but the marriage was not a success. She developed a new career first as an artist and then as a journalist and travel-writer, succeeding Tom Trollope in 1886 as Rome correspondent of *The Standard*. Retiring in 1898, she joined her sister Fanny in Calcot, later moving with her to Southsea where she died.

TERNAN, Frances Eleanor (1802–1873), née JARMAN, was the daughter of the theatrical prompter (roughly equivalent to a director today) John Jarman and his wife Maria, a leading provincial actress. Fanny Jarman made her provincial début in Bath in 1815 and her London one at Covent Garden in 1827. In 1834 she married a noted Irish actor-manager Thomas Ternan and at once set off with him for an extensive tour of the United States. After returning to England in 1837 they acted both in London and in the provinces and had two more daughters, Maria and Ellen. Widowed in 1846, Fanny consolidated her reputation as a fine Shakespearean actress while working with the leading actor-managers of the day, Macready, Phelps and Charles Kean, and keeping together her family of three actress daughters. She, Maria and Ellen acted with Dickens's Amateur Company in 1857. She finally retired from the stage in 1866, after which she seems to have resided mainly with her daughter Ellen until after Dickens's death when she joined her middle daughter Maria in Oxford.

TROLLOPE, Frances Eleanor (Fanny) née TERNAN (1835–1913), began her professional life as an 'infant phenomenon', making her London début in 1843. From 1849 onwards she concentrated on singing rather than acting and gave her first concert in 1853. Sustained success in this career eluded her, however, and in 1857 Dickens paid for her to go to Florence, chaperoned by her mother, to further her musical education. In Florence she became acquainted with Dickens's friend Thomas Trollope and his family. After Trollope's wife's death in 1865 she returned to Florence as companion-governess to his little daughter and married him the following year. By this time she was concentrating on a career as a novelist, which Dickens did his best to foster by serialising four of her stories in *All The Year Round* between 1866 and 1869. After being widowed in 1892 she joined Ellen and her family in Calcot before a final move to Southsea, where first Maria and then Ellen, also widowed, joined her.

WINTER, Maria, née BEADNELL (1811–87), was the third and youngest daughter of George Beadnell, a City banker. Dickens met her about 1830 and soon fell passionately in love. He remained infatuated for three or four years, an experience on which he drew in 1849 when describing David's courtship of Dora in *David Copperfield*. Maria had many admirers and tormented Dickens by sometimes seeming to return his love and at other times behaving with cold indifference. After three years of such treatment Dickens with a heavy heart abandoned all hope of winning her and two years later became engaged to Catherine Hogarth. He appears to have seen very little, if anything, of Maria over the next twenty-two years, though he kept in touch with her father and must surely have heard about her marriage in 1845 to Henry Winter, a Finsbury saw-mill manager, by whom she had a daughter Ella. When she wrote to Dickens out of the blue in February 1855 his emotional life was in a state of considerable turbulence and he responded to her with passionate eagerness, writing with a seemingly total recall of all the details of his courtship of her so many years before. She seems to have responded by saying that she really had loved him and this excited him further. But his fantasy that she would now be just as she was then was completely shattered the moment they met. He subsequently depicted her as the good-hearted but fat and foolish Flora Finching in *Little Dorrit*. Maria seems to have taken no offence, however, and maintained her friendship with him as best she could for the rest of his life. Winter after his bankruptcy in 1859 embarked on a new career as a Church of England priest. He died in 1871 and Maria lived on for another sixteen years, keeping in touch with Georgina Hogarth and preserving Dickens's letters to her while she treasured her memories of the days when she had been so passionately loved by him.

WRIGHT, Thomas (1859–1936), was born and lived all his life in Olney, Buckinghamshire, where he established a very successful school. His first book, *The Town of Cowper or the Literary and Historical Associations of Olney and its Neighbourhood*, appeared in 1886 and he went on to publish a number of biographies. His *Life of William Cowper* appeared in 1892 and was followed by lives of Defoe (1894) and Walter Pater (1907). He was a leading figure in the establishment of the Cowper Museum in the poet's former home in Olney, and was also an indefatigable founder of literary societies including the Cowper Society and the Blake Society. His autobiography *Thomas Wright of Olney* was published posthumously. For an illuminating discussion of Wright's investigative methods as a biographer, see Laurel Brake, *Print in Transition 1850–1910: Studies in Media and Book History* (London, 2001).

Select bibliography

Ackroyd, Peter, *Dickens* (London, 1990).

Adrian, Arthur, *Georgina Hogarth and the Dickens Circle* (London, 1957).

Aylmer, Felix, *Dickens Incognito* (London, 1959).

Bechhofer Roberts, C. E. ('Ephesian'), *This Side Idolatry: A Novel* (London, 1928).

Bigelow, John, *Retrospections of an Active Life*, 3 vols (New York, 1909).

Bredsdorff, Elias, *Hans Christian Andersen and Charles Dickens: A Friendship and its Dissolution* (Cambridge, 1956).

Dickens, Charles, *The Letters of Charles Dickens*, ed. Mamie Dickens and Georgina Hogarth, 2 vols (London, 1880); vol. 3 (London, 1882); rev. ed. in one vol. (London, 1893).

Dickens, Charles, *The Letters of Charles Dickens*, ed. Walter Dexter, 3 vols (Bloomsbury, The Nonesuch Press, 1938).

Dickens, Charles, *The Letters of Charles Dickens*, British Academy/Pilgrim Edition, 12 vols (Oxford, 1965–2002).

Forster, John, *The Life of Charles Dickens*, 3 vols (London, 1872–4).

Forster, John, *The Life of Charles Dickens*, ed. J. W. T. Ley (London, 1928).

Gordan, John D., 'The Secret of Dickens' Memoranda', in *Bookman's Holiday: Notes and Studies Written and Gathered in Tribute to Harry Miller Lyndenberg* (New York, 1943).

[Hotten, John Camden, and Taverner, H. T.], *Charles Dickens: The Story of His Life* (London, 1870).

Hunt, Cecil, *Ink in My Veins: literary reminiscences* (London, 1948).

Johnson Edgar, *Charles Dickens: His Tragedy and Triumph*, 2 vols (New York, 1952).

Kingsmill, Hugh, *The Sentimental Journey. A Life of Charles Dickens* (London, 1934).

Kitton, F. G., *Dickens by Pen and Pencil* (London, 1890).

Kitton, F. G., *Dickensiana: A Bibliography of the Literature Relating to Charles Dickens and his Writings* (London, 1886).

Lehmann, R. C. (ed.), *Charles Dickens as Editor, Being Letters Written by Him to William Henry Wills His Sub-Editor* (London, 1912).

Longley, Katharine M., 'The Real Ellen Ternan', *The Dickensian*, vol. 81 (London, 1985).

Maurois, André, *Dickens* (London, 1935).

Morley, Malcolm, 'The Theatrical Ternans', *The Dickensian*, vols. 54–57 (London, 1958–61).

Muggeridge, Malcolm, *The Thirties: 1930–1940 in Great Britain* (London, 1967).

Nayder, Lillian, *The Other Dickens. A Life of Catherine Dickens* (Ithaca and London, 2011).

Nisbet, Ada, *Dickens and Ellen Ternan* (Berkeley and Los Angeles, 1952).

Parker, David, and Slater, Michael, 'The Gladys Storey Papers', *The Dickensian*, vol. 76 (London, 1980).

Sala, George Augustus, *Letters of George Augustus Sala to Edmund Yates*, ed. Judy Mckenzie, Victorian Fiction Research Guides 19/20, Dept of English, University of Queensland (Brisbane, 1993).

Staples, Leslie C., 'Ellen Ternan – Some Letters', *The Dickensian*, vol. 61 (London, 1965).

Storey, Gladys, *Dickens and Daughter* (London, 1939).

Straus, Ralph, *Dickens: A Portrait in Pencil* (London, 1928).

Thackeray, W. M., *The Letters and Private Papers of William Makepeace Thackeray*, ed. Gordon N. Ray, 4 vols (London, 1945).

Tomalin, Claire, *The Invisible Woman: The Story of Nelly Ternan and Charles Dickens* (London, 1990; London [Penguin ed.], 1991).

Tomalin, Claire, *Charles Dickens: A Life* (London, 2012).

Wagenknecht, Edward, *Dickens and the Scandalmongers* (Norman, Oklahoma, 1965).

Ward, Adolphus, *Charles Dickens* (London, 1882).

Wilson, Edmund, *The Wound and the Bow* (Oxford, 1941).

Wright, Thomas, *The Life of Charles Dickens* (London, 1935).

Wright, Thomas, *Thomas Wright of Olney* (London, 1936).

For reference

DeVries, Duane, *General Studies of Charles Dickens and His Writings and Collected Editions of His Works: An Annotated Bibliography. Vol.2: Autobiographical Writings, Letters, Obituaries, Reminiscences, Biographies* (New York, 2010).

Schlicke, Paul (ed.), *The Oxford Companion to Charles Dickens. Anniversary Edition* (Oxford, 2011).

Archival

Dexter, Walter. Letters to the Comte de Suzannet, 1931–1944. Charles Dickens Museum.

Katharine M. Longley Papers. Senate House Library, University of London.

Kate Perugini, Correspondence with George Bernard Shaw. British Library.

Gladys Storey Papers. Charles Dickens Museum.

Thomas Wright Papers. Charles Dickens Museum.

Index